Who Cares About Phone Calls?

All Photos by IU Athletics

July 2012

Edited by Tara Hayden

2012 SIX TWENTYTWO PUBLISHING COMPANY All Rights Reserved

ISBN: 978-0-9882984-0-8

ISBN 978-0-9882984-0-8

9 780988 298408

For Liam, that he experiences all the highs of Indiana basketball as he grows up that I did. And none of the lows.

Thank you to all the people who helped me become the Hoosier fan I am today, my parents Steve and Donna Taylor, my brother, Michael, with whom I relived all the best IU moments on the hoop in the driveway, my cousins, Kim and Carol Fisher, who taught me about fanaticism and team loyalty through word and deed, Brian Fisher, who turned his painters cap inside out and backwards with me one March night in 1987. Thank you to Sam Weller who first put the idea into my head that I could write something as ambitious as a book and helped guide me through this process. Thank you to the Summer Novelist's / Writer's Club, being a part of a group of talented and dedicated writers sharing the struggle of getting the work done, day by day, was an unbelievable help during drafts two through five, as this book finally took shape. Thank you to Adam Bowling, frequently my audience of one. Thank you to Deana Labriola, Sam Spicer and Brad Hubbard who read very early drafts and were kind enough not to tell me that what I had written wasn't a book so much as giant notebook of disjointed nonsense. I figured that out eventually. And finally, to my wife, Laura for allowing me the time work on this hour after hour, day after day, year after year.

Prelude: On "We"

I don't know when I first read *A Season on the Brink*, John (Junior) Feinstein's book about the year he spent with Bob Knight and the Hoosiers, but I know it wasn't when it came out in 1986. It was a bit above my fourth-grade reading level, but when I finally did read it—probably when I was in high school or college—I was struck with one thought beyond how great a book it is, which was how much better it would have been if he'd written it during the 1986-1987 season instead of the 1985-1986 season. To have followed that team during our run to a championship instead of the year before... what I wouldn't have given to have read *that* book.

I started blogging about IU basketball to give myself an outlet, as I no longer lived in Indiana and my outlets for discussing the Hoosiers were few. As the 2007-2008 season approached, I looked at our lineup, lead by senior big man, DJ White, a player with the Big Ten Player of the Year potential, with sophomore guard Armon Bassett, a player who had shown the potential as a freshman to be a dominant Big Ten guard as he developed, in the backcourt alongside incoming five-star freshman Eric "EJ" Gordon and thought *this might be the year we get back to the Final Four.*

Considering how I felt after reading *A Season on the Brink*, I thought this would be a great chance to chronicle a season that was more likely to end in the Final Four than against Cleveland State in the opening round of the NCAA tournament.

It was with expectations of victory that I set out to write this book. The season I ended up following was the most destructive season in the history of Indiana basketball, a season with repercussions that would be felt for years to come. It wasn't the success I expected it to be, but it wasn't uninteresting.

This is a book about a basketball program in peril, a coach who said that Indiana basketball was bigger than one person and then proceeded to show just how much damage one person can do, and a fan base struggling through an identity crisis. But mostly it's a book about me. They say write what you know, right?

It's about how I responded to the events that led to Kelvin Sampson's midseason resignation, and how I viewed everything he said that season through the prism of how it ended. It was a personal journey for me, watching and listening to the games, reading the press, and listening to the press conferences and coach's radio show. What follows is not objective. It's highly subjective, as it should be because I'm not a reporter with access to practices, meetings, the locker room, and the bench. I'm a fan with access to TV, newspapers, and the Internet.

There are two things about the way I wrote this that I want state up front. First, I am a product of my time. My knowledge of Indiana basketball extends through my own timeline. I'm the Dr. Sam Beckett of Indiana basketball. I can go back in time, but only as far back as my own birth. You'll see few if any references to George McGinnis or the Van Arsdale twins.[1]

Being a product of my time means that I view everything through the filter of my constant exposure to and love of pop culture. This includes Indiana basketball. You can expect to see references to *M*A*S*H*; Julius Caesar; Rocky; The Karate Kid; WWF Wrestling; The Simpsons; Seinfeld* ; Harrison Ford; Tom Cruise; and Tom Hanks; among others. Some of them will be well drawn out and explained, others, like the above reference to the main character in and primary conceit of *Quantum Leap*, will be thrown out there with the expectation that you'll either know what I'm talking about, look it up, or just ignore it and move on.

The second is something that is likely to bother half the sports viewing audience, which is that I refer to this team in the first person plural. The use of "we" in relation to the team you root for is a bone of contention for some sports fans. I use it throughout and here's why: There is a relationship between the fan and the team. There always has been. The fan and the team have entered into an agreement. The entire sports relationship is based on this agreement, though it has never been written down, signed, or even spoken aloud.

It is a symbiotic relationship; without the team there are no fans, and without the fan there is no need for a team. They each fulfill, for the other, important needs. The team provides the fan with, at the basest level, entertainment and distraction, but much more than that, the team provides the fan with a sense of community, of belonging. They also allow

---

[1] In fact I'm pretty sure that was the only one.

the fan to experience the glory of victory without having to put in the work. In turn, the fans provide the team with support, both financial and emotional, as well as a sense of purpose. Every team plays to win for themselves, but also for the fans.

But this is not a relationship without expectations. The fan expects the team to win. That is a given, but on a more fundamental level, the fan expects the team to represent him. If a fan sees the team as an extension of himself (and he must in order to gain any sense of pride or accomplishment from the successes of the team), then he expects the team to live up to the ideals he has for himself. No one wants to be disappointed with his own actions. The same holds true for his larger self, his team.

Through the course of this book I put a lot of responsibility on the fan. I expect a lot of the fan, just as the fan places a lot of expectations on the teams. When the team is not meeting the expectations of the fan, the fan has the right and I would even argue the responsibility to do his part to help the team meet those expectations. When the fans fail in that responsibility, it can have disastrous consequences. The fan can't go on the court and play, or go in the locker room and coach, but the culture of a program is as important as the product on the court and the fans play a huge role in that culture.

I view the team as an extension of myself. They represent the hopes from my childhood when I would watch players I looked up to wear the Indiana uniform, and dream of a day when I would be one of them. Watching your favorite team involves a certain level of wish fulfillment. When they win, I feel like I've won. I feel good. I can talk trash to my friends. When they lose, I feel like I lost. I'm mad, or disappointed. I have to suffer the trash talking.

It's because I identify with the team and have positive and negative emotional responses to their successes and failures that I bother to cheer for them. I don't play, coach, or put in the work, but I experience a real emotional response at the outcome of a game. For better or worse, we are tied together throughout the season. And that's why I use the word "we."

I can accept that you may not agree with that, but know that I don't use it without forethought. Its use is intentional and its meaning is clear. I am a part of Indiana basketball. It is a part of me. And if you're reading this, I'm assuming it's a part of you, too.

Parole Board chairman: "They've got a name for people like you H.I. That name is called recidivism."

Parole Board member: "Repeat offender!"

Parole Board chairman: "Not a pretty name, is it H.I.?"

H.I.: "No, sir. That's one bonehead name, but that ain't me anymore."

Parole Board chairman: "You're not just telling us what we want to hear?"

H.I.: "No, sir, no way."

Parole Board member: "Cuz we just want to hear the truth."

H.I.: "Well, then I guess I am telling you what you want to hear."

Parole Board chairman: "Boy, didn't we just tell you not to do that?"

H.I.: "Yes, sir."

Parole Board chairman: "Okay, then."

—*Raising Arizona*

Chapter One: Beginnings

Sometimes the way a thing begins tells you everything you need to know. On the other hand, sometimes, like the details of Dr. Evil's life, it is quite inconsequential. Sometimes the kid you meet at the church fete who has a guitar strung upside down so he can play *20 Flight Rock* left-handed is just some kid, and sometimes it's the beginning of the greatest band in the history of rock 'n' roll. Whether the details of how a thing begins prove to be important and telling to the outcome or whether it's all just nonsense, when we are at the beginning of the story, well, dude, we just don't know.

Raising Arizona has one of those beginnings that tells you everything you need to know about the story that's about to unfold. We meet H.I. McDonnough, our protagonist, as he is shoved in front of a camera for his mug shot. Seconds later we meet Edwina, a corrections officer and a flower, who instructs him to "Turn to the right!" H.I. attends counseling sessions with other cons, where we meet Gale and Evelle Stokes (finest pair that ever broke and entered), two of our main antagonists. H.I. is released, knocks over another convenience store, gets arrested, tries to console Ed (whose Fai-ants has left her) and is later released. He tries to "fly straight but it ain't easy with that sumbitch Reagan in the White House." He's arrested again, proposes to Ed, is released, and they promptly marry.

H.I. gets a job in a factory and a starter home in suburban Tempe and he and Ed begin their efforts to have a family, but sadly Ed's insides are a rocky place where his seed can find no purchase. Her level of distress is such that when the news breaks that Florence Arizona, wife of Nathan Arizona (and hell, you know who he is), has been graced with quintuplets she sees what perhaps is the solution to all their problems and the answer to all their prayers.

We meet the main characters, learn their problem, can infer their solution, and even meet the largest obstacles to that solution, all before the opening credits. It may be the greatest beginning to any film ever for providing the set up so succinctly, with *Raiders of the Lost Ark* coming in a close second.

On the opposite end of the spectrum is the beginning of almost every James Bond movie ever made. They're exciting; things blow up, people are chased and shot, and women are frequently half-naked, but seldom does all of this actually introduce the plot or even the bad guy. I'm not calling Albert R. Broccoli or Ian Fleming an idiot, but if the phrase "full of sound and fury, signifying nothing" ever applied, it does to the opening sequences of Bond movies. So, when you get right down to it, Shakespeare was the one calling them idiots.

The best[2] of these is *Goldeneye*, where 007 jumps off the side of a

---

[2] And by best, I mean the most ridiculous and hard to believe.

cliff after a plane, catches up with the plane, climbs inside, and flies away to safety. In your face Galileo! At the end of these fantastic action sequences we enter the realm of the surrealistic title sequence and the movie begins. We were entertained, but we are no closer to an understanding of the film than when we were applying the fake butter topping to our popcorn in the lobby.

My beginnings as an Indiana basketball fan are much more the *Raising Arizona* variety, only with less prison time. I was born in December 1975, in the middle of the last perfect season in college basketball. I was raised in Clarksville, Indiana, right on the border with Kentucky, in the heart of a triple-threat match of basketball fandom. Though I was too young to realize it until the mid-1980s, I was growing up in a golden era of college basketball, in the Fertile Crescent where the Ohio River was the Tigris and, oh, I don't know, Silver Creek was the Euphrates.

In 1976, IU completed the last perfect season in college basketball with a defeat over Michigan in the NCAA National Championship game. In 1978 Kentucky won the title with players who were being paid, but more on that later. In 1979, Indiana State, led by Larry Bird, lost the championship to Magic Johnson and Michigan State in one of the most important, non-IU national championships ever played. In 1980, Louisville captured their first title, followed in 1981 by Isiah Thomas and IU winning Bob Knight his second crown. Louisville won again in 1986 and Keith Smart hit the greatest shot in an NCAA Championship game ever to upend Syracuse and give IU its third title in 12 years.

I grew up not only to great basketball success, but in an area where the other major schools were having great success. This kind of environment bred passionate fans and heated rivalries.

I've often heard people say that they were born in the wrong era.

This mostly seems to apply to women who read a lot of Jane Austen novels or teenagers who like the 1960s way too much. I was born at the right time. Paul Simon might as well have been singing about me. Not only was I born in the right place and time to be brought up a rabid IU fan, I was born at the best moment to become a full media consumer. Not only was the winter of 1975-1976 during *the perfect season* it was the first season of *Saturday Night Live*. I am old enough to remember when we had three channels to choose from. I remember when we got cable for the first time and I sat there for hours watching Nickelodeon, waiting for *You Can't Do That On Television* to come on.

My generation is marked by the invention of the VCR and the launch of MTV. We were the first to grow up with choices. We could choose from over 100 channels and we could time-shift our viewing, choosing to record our shows and watch them at our leisure. We could bring movies home. And while none of these things was true for our parents, they became commonplace to us.

Mine was a childhood of Saturday morning cartoons (*Schoolhouse Rock!*, *GI Joe*, *Transformers*, and *He-Man*), TV during dinner (mostly reruns of *M*A*S*H* and the most boring thing of all, local nightly news), and evenings of *Cheers*; *Family Ties*; *The A-Team*, *The Dukes of Hazzard*, and later *The Simpsons*; *Beverly Hills, 90210*, *The X-Files*; and too many others to name. There were drawers full of VHS tapes with hundreds of movies to choose from and blank tapes ready to record *The Cosby Show* every week.

When there wasn't TV, there was music. I got my first cassette player in 1982 with the release of *Thriller*, but we still had albums, 45s, and a reel-to-reel deck. My father's love of doo-wop and oldies and my mother's love of Barbara Streisand (*Woman in Love*, *Funny Girl* ... that kind of stuff) permeated the house and my consciousness. I was almost in high school when I got my first CD player and Walkman.

I mark the moments in my childhood by two things, Indiana championships and the media. I was a four-and-a-half when *The Empire Strikes Back* was released, the first movie I remember seeing in the theater. I was in fourth grade when Eddie Murphy had a girl that wanted to *Party All The Time and* they wheeled a TV into our classroom so my classmates and I could watch the coverage of the Challenger disaster. I was in fifth grade when Steve Alford and Daryl Thomas were seniors and we won the title in New Orleans. I was in eighth grade when I watched the Berlin Wall collapse live on TV to a soundtrack of *New Kids on the Block* and *Milli Vanilli.*

I think this is true of most people my age. Maybe not the Indiana championships part, though I'm sure that's true of Hoosier fans my age, but the growth of media that coincides with my growth and development has given me the lenses through which I see the world. I share these childhood experiences with millions of people my age. We experienced them together, though we never knew each other[3].

At the end of the movie *Grand Canyon,* Steve Martin's character, Davis, is pontificating to Mack, Kevin Kline's character, and he says something that just about nails my view of the world, which is "You haven't seen enough movies. All of life's riddles are answered in the movies."

Consequently, every year I want IU's exhibition games to be like the introduction to *Raising Arizona.* I want to learn something about our new players. I want to get a feel for our shortcomings. I want to establish

---

[3] One of my best friends met her husband on match.com and one of the things that they immediately clicked on was Denise's failed efforts to make Theo a shirt as cool as his Gordon Gartrell. They grew up in different parts of the country, in different faith backgrounds, and they knew no one in common, but they both had this childhood experience to bond over. For my wife and I, it was the movie Clue.

a baseline against which I can accurately set my expectations.

What I end up getting, most of the time, is a blowout that doesn't tell me much, but since it's the only data I have, I want to make it mean everything. I want *Raising Arizona,* but I always end up with a James Bond movie.

The exhibition games in November 2007 had a different feel than past exhibition games for a number of reasons. The first was that most Hoosier fans were eagerly awaiting the start to a season with more championship promise than any since 1992. DJ was entering his senior year and looked to be a dominant force in the Big Ten, and our freshman class was led by Eric Gordon, the most heralded recruit to suit up for IU since Jared Jeffries. Hopes were high. Expectations were great. But the expectations for the season and the desire to see EJ were not the biggest story. Head coach, Kelvin Sampson had seen to that.

In March 2006, when IU hired Sampson he was under sanctions that his previous employer, the University of Oklahoma, had imposed in response to 577 impermissible phone calls he had made to recruits over a five-year-span when seemingly no one at the university was paying the slightest attention to his actions or to the rules. Indiana University chose to keep the sanctions in place that pertained directly to Sampson until the end of June 2007. Those sanctions were as follows: Either Sampson or the director of men's basketball operations would meet with the director of compliance weekly to make sure Sampson was following the rules. Under normal circumstances, a coaching staff is allowed to call a recruit once a month during the recruit's sophomore and junior years and twice a week during their senior year. Sampson's staff was allowed half of that and was limited to four days of off-campus recruiting.

The NCAA Committee on Infractions imposed additional

sanctions that prohibited Sampson from making any recruiting phone calls or being present when his staff made phone calls. These penalties were in place from March 29, 2006 to May 24, 2007.

Indiana University agreed to file a report detailing compliance with these sanctions to the Committee on Infractions by the end of August 2007. That report is a fantastic read, if you like legalese, and it was the source for what you're about to read. That deadline was extended to October 3, 2007, after the university informed the Committee that it was investigating some three-way phone calls involving Sampson, assistant coach Rob Senderoff, and recruits that were contrary to the sanctions, and asked for more time to complete the investigation.

The university discovered a number of violations to the sanctions in place and the NCAA rules. It was discovered that Senderoff, despite submitting monthly reports stating that he did not use his home phone for recruiting purposes, had in fact made numerous recruiting phone calls from his home phone. Assistant coach Jeff Meyer was also found to have made "10 recruiting calls from home, several of which were contrary to the sanctions and one that was contrary to NCAA rules." There were 27 three-way phone calls placed between March 29, 2006 and May 24, 2007, all of which were contrary to the sanctions in place prohibiting Sampson from "making any phone calls that relate in any way to recruiting or being present when members of his staff make such calls." Of those 27 calls, between 10 and 18 of them involved recruits.[4] Of the phone calls Senderoff placed from home, 101 of them were impermissible, 99 were contrary to the sanctions, and 34 were NCAA violations. Of the calls Meyer made from home, four were impermissible and contrary to sanctions and one was an NCAA violation.

---

[4] A specific clarification was received from the NCAA about three-way phone calls on June 13, 2006, confirming that they were in fact prohibited.

The explanation for the three-way calls was that A.) The cell reception at Sampson's home was not good and frequently he would be on permissible calls with recruits when the call would be dropped. He would either text the recruit to call him back or contact an assistant to have them contact the recruit to remind them to call Sampson back, as he could not call them, and B.) Occasionally Senderoff would call a recruit, talk to them for a few minutes, put them on hold, call Sampson and patch the calls together, acting, as he said, as an "operator." He claimed that he never participated in any of these conversations, but merely connected the calls and waited on the line to disconnect them when they were done talking. Senderoff told the university that he viewed this kind of activity as a gray area. How gray? Charcoal.

Sampson's recidivist nature was revealed to the public when the university released its Report to the Committee on Infractions on October 14, 2007, the morning after Hoosier Hysteria. Portions of Hoosier Hysteria were broadcast the previous evening on the new Big Ten Network. That Friday night the Hoosier faithful were excited and ready for a championship run, but by Saturday morning so many of us felt like our game of *Sink the Bismarck!* had gotten out of control the night before.

And while we were all worshipping the porcelain god, IU's athletic director Rick Greenspan was making a sacrifice to appease the angry and vengeful NCAA gods, which involved more sanctions. As a result, the school forfeited one scholarship for the 2008-2009 basketball season, reduced the number of coaches allowed to be involved in recruiting through July 31, 2008, and prohibited Senderoff from calling any recruits, participating in any off-campus recruiting, or using his phone for anything other than voting for the next *American Idol.*[5] Senderoff and Meyer

[5] He just LOVED David Archuleta.

forfeited any bonuses and Sampson gave up a $500,000 pay raise. Sampson was limited to four off-campus recruiting days during the fall period and 10 recruiting days from October 5, 2007 to July 31, 2008, and his ability to call recruits was again limited.

On October 30, 2007, Senderoff resigned his position as assistant coach and was replaced by former IU player and assistant coach Dan Dakich, whose perpetual claim to fame is his defensive effort against Michael Jordan in Jordan's final college game. Dakich had just returned to IU as the director of basketball operations after a 10-year stint as the head coach for Bowling Green State University.

When Sampson was hired, the decision was met with some pretty vocal opposition, most notably from former Hoosiers Kent Benson and Ted Kitchel who could have warned us about Sampson, if only they spoke Hovitos. And when news broke about Sampson's controversial dealings at IU, *Indianapolis Star* columnist Bob Kravitz waited almost 24 full hours after the story broke to call for a house cleaning.

While the reaction from the Hoosiers' fan base was swift, the opposition to Sampson was far from universal, as many fans thought his actions didn't seem like that big of a deal. I was somewhere in the middle. It concerned me that he was getting busted for committing the same type of offenses that he had committed before, but I wasn't ready to tear up all the flowers and salt the Earth so nothing would ever grow again. It's one thing to make a mistake. It's another thing to repeat that mistake after being punished for it once already. I feel the same way about Pam Anderson marrying Tommy Lee. Fine, you married him, he beat you and gave you Hepatitis C, but at least you got out of…Wait. What? You married him again? And then divorced him and married Kid Rock? At this point Coach Sampson had remarried Tommy Lee. If he followed this up by marrying Kid Rock, that would be far more than I could forgive.

18

Indiana University, while taking concerns about Sampson's reputation and history of cheating seriously, stated in its Report to the Committee on Infractions that with "so few impermissible calls involving Sampson (10 to 18) out of the thousands of recruiting calls made from May 2006 through May 2007, this could not have been a purposeful plan to circumvent the sanction."

During his weekly press conference leading up to the North Alabama exhibition game on November 4, Coach Sampson refused to answer any questions about his repeated transgressions. He wouldn't address it, he said, because it was an open investigation by the NCAA and he didn't want to do anything to interfere with that. It was a good enough reason, and one that seemed plausible. And it was probably true that he shouldn't have spoken about it because of the investigation, but at its core that was nothing more than misdirection. "Pay no attention to the man behind the curtain!"

Sampson was delusional if he thought that he could topsy-turvy the situation just by refusing to answer questions. He needed one of two things to happen for this to be forced from people's minds; either time for the focus to shift to the team, or some catastrophic event to push this off the front page. He needed a Gary Condit.

Remember Gary Condit? Don't feel bad if you don't. There's a very good reason for that. But before you forgot completely who he was he was, for one summer, the only thing you cared about. Gary Condit was a Democratic Congressman from California's 18th, who spent the entire summer of 2001 as the only story on the planet. On May, 1 2001 an intern for the Federal Bureau of Prisons named Chandra Levy, who was from Condit's home district, disappeared.

It turned out that Condit had been having an affair with Levy and was almost immediately thrust into the public's consciousness as the only person who could have possibly killed or disappeared Levy. Condit and Levy were the only thing anyone seemed to care about, and eventually, hoping to gain some control over the story that was ruining his life, Condit gave an interview to Connie Chung, an idea Bob Knight might have tried to talk him out of, if only he'd been asked. It did nothing to convince anyone that he was anything but guilty.

People thought he was being evasive. He was still the main story on almost every news outlet and had been front page scandal news for over two months. What Condit, who has long since been cleared of all suspicion in the death and disappearance of Chandra Levy, needed more than anything to save his career was to get out of the media spotlight. He needed to get off the front page.

He must have made this wish using a cursed monkey's paw because he got exactly what he needed, in a way he never could have wanted when New York and Washington, D.C. were attacked on the morning of September 11, 2001. Suddenly, no one cared about Gary Condit and the name Chandra Levy disappeared from the pages of the newspapers and the consciousness of the public.

But Kelvin Sampson didn't get the Condit he so desperately needed. We didn't even get to the tip-off before John Laskowski, former IU "Super-Sub" and broadcasting constant, brought it up. There was no way Laz could avoid leading with the biggest story surrounding Indiana basketball, as it certainly placed the game in its current context, but do you think there was anyone watching an IU versus North Alabama exhibition game who didn't know about this story? Roughly the same number of men in this country that ain't seen Madonna's bosoms? Yeah, that's what I think, too.

I don't want to suggest that he should have ignored it, but if there was nothing new to report, and 98 percent of your audience (and I am being generous giving North Alabama 2 percent of the market share for this game)[6], what's the point of bringing it up? It's tantamount to reminding everyone that a basket is worth two points and you have to bounce the ball if you want to move while you have it.

If all you saw was the final score of the North Alabama game, I imagine it would have seemed just about right, a phenomenon that would hold true for much of the season. We won 121-76, but we might not have covered the point spread. Still, the outcome of this game was never in doubt. The same can be said for the outcome of the second exhibition game against UNC Pembroke played six days later, which we won 111-62.

But I don't watch our exhibition games to see the outcomes, just as I don't watch James Bond openings to get to the credit sequence. I watch 007 to see insane stunts and explosions. I watch IU exhibition games to get to know the team. I expect us to win, just as I expect the credits of a Bond film to eventually roll.

So, now I'd met this team, but did I know anything about them worth knowing? Sure, a few things. We were a very athletic team with tremendous offensive ability. Our guards could shoot, drive, and create their own shots, and DJ could get it done in the post. Still, we were a bad defensive team. We gave up 39 points in the first half to North Alabama and 35 points against Pembroke. The benchmark I've always used for first half defensive production is 35 points, which I took from a sign hanging in the Indiana locker room in 1997. If you can keep your opponent below 35 points in the first half, it is indicative of a good defensive performance. That number should be adjusted down to 30 in an exhibition, and we

---

[6] Packer Method: See Chapter Five for a full discourse on the Packer Method.

could not hold a much weaker opponent under this particular Mendoza line.

We couldn't stop either team in transition. And our half-court defense wasn't any better. Our help-side rotation was slow and we had numerous possessions in which our players were facing the sideline or the baseline as the ball was driven right at the back of their heads. And on the occasions in which we didn't give up easy transition baskets, or completely uncontested drives to the basket, we played decent defense only to give up easy points at the end of the possession.

We didn't play poorly, but we played inconsistently. We were the *Kids in the Hall* of college basketball teams. At times we were transcendent (groin-grabbingly so), while at other times we did things that were so awful they shouldn't be shown on Canadian television.

What then should we take from these exhibition games and the events surrounding them? How much of what we saw was predictive of what is to come and how much was just chaff?

Time would tell. Maybe Jordan Crawford, a freshman guard from Hargrave Military Academy who averaged nearly 20 points a game in his senior season, would shoot 10-11 every other game. Maybe freshman phenom, Eric Gordon, and senior big man DJ White would be the best inside-outside combo in basketball this season. Maybe we'd play the entire season under a cloud of suspicion and apprehension because the NCAA was dangling a Damocleasian sword over our heads. Maybe we'd put freshmen into the game in the second half who would score 20+ points every night, as Brandon McGee did. Maybe we'd give up easy baskets because of sloppy fundamentals, but make up for it with our athleticism in every game all season long.

Maybe it was time to move on to the games that count.

Interlude One: I'm the Doctor

In 1966, with William Hartnell set to depart his role as the titular character in the BBC science fiction series, *Doctor Who*, the creators needed a way to continue the series without the lead actor. The solution they came up with was that the Doctor, because he was a Time Lord, an alien race that traveled through time and space observing and oftentimes becoming involved in the lives and events of those times, when he died, he could be reborn, or regenerate in another body. This allowed them to hire a new actor to play the Doctor and because he was in a new body, the Doctor could have completely different mannerisms, likes, dislikes, and aspects of his personality. Every actor to subsequently play the role of the Doctor has put his own stamp on the role, breathing new life into the series.

Each coach who dons the title of Head Basketball Coach at Indiana University has taken the press conference and infused it with his own personality, making it his own in much the same way David Tennant's Doctor was very different from Christopher Eccleston's or Tom Baker's. Bob Knight used the press conferences mostly to skewer the media. According to John (Junior) Feinstein in *A Season on the Brink*, "Knight almost never told the press exactly what he thought, but that hardly made him unusual." Knight was funny and caustic and his press conferences took on that same personality. He famously went on tirades, mocked reporters by using his drinking glass to peer into the future, demonstrated what he thought a "game face" looked like and tried to squeeze blood out of a whip. Bob Knight press conferences must have been 75 percent of the motivation behind the existence of ESPNews and the decision to cover postgame press conferences.

Mike Davis, on the other hand, was uncomfortable talking to the media so his press conferences were equally uncomfortable, and one got the feeling that if he could he would never hold another one.

Sampson was a bit of an enigma, and his press conferences were full of confusing, incomprehensible, and occasionally awkward statements that were maybe better left unsaid. There was no doubt that he was the new Doctor, for better or worse.

Take for instance, our first introduction to Jordan Crawford and his 10-11 shooting night against North Alabama. Crawford looked fearless with the ball and ready to shoot it from anywhere on the court, bringing to mind comparisons with the recently graduated streak-shooter, Rod Wilmont. In response to a question about that comparison, Sampson said, "There will never be another Rod Wilmont. Jordan can pass and dribble."

Sampson was clearly joking when he said this, but it died an excruciating death, hanging in the air in a room of shocked journalists. It was greeted with a few polite but uncomfortable chuckles and one reporter who said only, "Wow." On the "Michael Scott Inappropriateness Scale," that statement falls somewhere between the birthday card reading, "Let's hope the only downsizing this year is that someone downsizes your age" and "This is our receptionist, Pam. If you think she's cute now you should have seen her a couple of years ago!"

Our young team had shown an ability to shoot and a joyous embrace of the three-pointer that bordered on rapturous. When Sampson was asked whether he liked that kind of approach to the game and whether he thought 30 threes were too many, he said, "I don't mind threes as long as they go in. You shoot 30 threes, you're not making any, probably not a good idea, but if you shoot 30 and are making 18, I'd say they're pretty good shots."

This view of three-point shooting gave us our first real insight into

Sampson's mentality, the transitive property of quality: Three pointers = shots, made shots = good. Thus, made three-pointers = good shots. Or, put more simply: Successful outcome = good action. Ladies and gentlemen, the Sampson Syllogism. If Crawford dribbled into a double team and threw the ball over his head and it went in, by virtue of the Sampson Syllogism, this was a good shot. But, if DJ missed a layup, it was a bad shot. If you won you must have played well. If you lost you played poorly.

If Hoosier football coach Bill Lynch decided to punt on first down and we recovered a fumble for a touchdown, it was a good idea, but if he ran the ball on third and inches and was stopped, it was a bad idea. Or, if Sampson's coaching staff made over 600 impermissible phone calls to recruits and didn't get caught it was a good idea, but if they got caught it was a bad idea. See how simple that is?

Sampson laid the groundwork in these early press conferences for his major press conference themes of the year. Namely, "this is a young team" and his Pollyanna-like analysis of the games, starting with his statement "I thought the intensity on defense in the second half was a lot better." He showed from the start that he was perfectly willing to focus on a small portion of the game that was good, and explain the other parts by citing our youth. As he eventually did, in this strange trip through the rock 'n' roll hall of fame: "You know we're not the Bee Gees or the Temptations or the, um, um, The Doobie Brothers…." *I had no idea where he was going with this comparison, but I couldn't wait to find out.* "…[we're] young kids. I mean every coach that is playing a bunch of freshmen is just going to have to be patient with them."

It turns out he wasn't going anywhere.

Except back to the well.

Chapter Two: Eating Onions, Spotting Dimes

My grandma makes the best chocolate chip cookies you've ever tasted. I know everyone, if asked, says the same thing about their grandma's cookies. They mean it and are very sincere and certain in this belief. They're wrong. This is not just my biased opinion. To support my statement, I have the testimonies of people who are not her direct descendants who would come over to my house and ask if I had any "Grandma Cookies." Kids would come from miles around to sample my grandma's wares.

As an undergrad, I would return to Bloomington from weekend trips visiting my family and would receive at least one phone call in which the only words spoken on the other end of the line were "You got any Grandma Cookies?" People would stop by to grab a couple Grandma Cookies and run. No one would want to hang out and watch reruns of *227* with me. They just wanted to grab the *Pineapple Express* and go, either to nowhere or Quiznos.

What makes my grandma's cookies so good? In terms of the recipe, I have no idea. My theory is that there's a little bit of love in each cookie. What I do know is that they never disappointed. You never took a bite of a Grandma Cookie and said, "What the hell is that?!"

In a world of ups and downs, strikes and gutters, Grandma Cookies are a constant. Terrence Mann, had he tasted Grandma Cookies, would have been reminded of baseball. Daniel Faraday could led Desmond Hume through time travel with only Grandma Cookies to latch onto. People crave this kind of consistency. How many times have you heard an athlete or a sportscaster say they don't care how well the game is called, so long as the refs are consistent? But there are so few things that are consistently one thing or another. Even things that are generally considered to be great have moments of awful. For Elvis, it was every movie he ever made. For *Saturday Night Live*, there have been years of "Saturday Night Dead" headlines. Even God has had his moments. After all, he created Kentucky fans.

This is one of the reasons *The Peanuts* was so popular. Charles M. Schulz was a miserable prick. He must have been; look at all the things he did to Charlie Brown. He took every last bit of frustration he had about the world, all the hurt and rejection, all his feelings of being unpopular and unloved, and inflicted it on poor Charlie.

Schulz didn't bury the lead about how he planned to treat Charlie Brown. In the first ever *Peanuts* comic strip, two kids sat on a curb as Charlie Brown approached. The boy on the stoop said, "Here comes good ol' Charlie Brown!" And just after he passed them, the kid said, "Good ol' Charlie Brown, Yes, sir… how I hate him."

In the second strip Charlie gets punched in the face for no reason at all by a little girl skipping down the street. He was so lonely he called the operator and asked her to tell him a story. When a new girl moved into the neighborhood, Charlie could never make time with her because she had already gotten everything she needed from his dog. He spent years longing for the Little Redhead Girl, only to be rejected, repeatedly.

And Schulz wasn't content to punish this poor kid for everything that had ever gone wrong on ordinary days of the year. He made sure that Charlie would get no relief on any of the major holidays, either. On Valentine's Day he was the only kid who didn't get a valentine. On Halloween everyone else got candy, he got rocks. The girls used his oddly round head to practice drawing their Jack-O-Lanterns. And he was abused at Christmas and no one listened to him.

Lucy held that football for Charlie to kick and pulled it back at the last second Every. Single. Time. And people loved it. They ate up this child abuse for over 50 years, and if that wasn't enough, Schulz' three- or four-frame helpings of torture are rerun in papers across the country every day. And he's been dead since 2000!

There's an argument to be made that the *Peanuts* are a prime example of our love of schadenfreude. But mostly, I think people knew what they were going to get from Schulz and they found comfort and pleasure in that consistency.

There's a reason that McDonald's, Starbucks, Subway, Burger King, and every other chain restaurant thrives year after year. Hint: It's not quality. It's partially cost and convenience, but mostly it's because when you order a Big Mac in Delaware it's going to taste exactly the same way it tastes if you order it in Los Angeles. If it was cheap and convenient but a complete gamble on what you were going to be eating, no one would bother, which is why I'm no fan of heart-shaped boxes with assorted chocolates. Sometimes it's a caramel or a peanut butter chocolate, but all too often it's coconut and the risk of having to wash that taste out of my mouth keeps me away from any box without a detailed chart of flavor and position. It's why I would never buy Bertie Bott's Every Flavor Beans. Who wants to get vomit flavor?[7]

McDonald's knew long ago how important consistency of product and service were to their profitability, world domination, and inclusion in the Pentaverate, that in 1961 they went as far as to establish Hamburger University in Oak Brook, Illinois.

And in another nod to consistency, Starbucks closed down all of their stores nationwide for three hours on February 26, 2008, for what was billed as an emergency re-training of all of their baristas so that everyone knew how to make every drink in exactly the same way.

The drive for consistency is not limited to food chains. Target stores strive to provide consistency to the point where not only are all Target stores laid out in roughly the same way, but they even smell the same.

Terrence Mann, Daniel Faraday, *Peanuts* fans, baristas, and Bachelors of Hamburgerology would have absolutely loved watching this basketball team through the first three games of the 2007-2008 season.

Our final exhibition against UNC Pembroke was on November 10. We started playing UT-Chattanooga at 7:40 p.m. on November 12, roughly 40 minutes after Chattanooga started playing us. Here's a fun fact: Did you know that the big lead you had at the end of the last game does

---

[7] Yes, coconut and vomit are completely analogous.

not carry over to the start of your next game? We didn't.

Chattanooga jumped out to a 7-2 lead on the strength of two layups in a nine second span. We allowed an uncontested drive to the basket, turned the ball over on the inbounds and allowed another layup right after. We looked like the Washington Generals. Chattanooga ran the five-man weave at the top of the key. Then point guard Kevin Bridgewaters ran over to our bench with a bucket of water to throw on senior forward, Lance Stemler. It was filled with confetti! Hilarious.[8]

We rallied on the strength of our three-point and free throw shooting, as 17 of our first 25 points came from three-point baskets and free throws, to take a 25-18 lead, but our defense made it impossible to hold the lead. We frequently lost individual players, and, at times, the ball itself. We tried to fight over the top of double screens unsuccessfully, giving Chattanooga really good looks at the basket. Our transition defense allowed many layups. Our help-side defense was either slow or nonexistent, and we were being out hustled on both ends of the court. On some possessions we would play solid defense for 20 or more seconds only to completely break down and give up an uncontested shot. In other words, we were playing the exact same defense we played during the exhibition games.

We had no answer for Bridgewaters as he torched us for 14 points in the first half, but we continued to score easily. We went into halftime trailing by four points, 50-46, continuing our trend of giving up way too many first-half points.

The second half was a horse of a different color. At halftime, Sampson switched EJ's defensive assignment, putting him on

---

[8] I'll give you a second to get control of yourself. The confetti gag kills every time.

Bridgewaters, who didn't score another point the rest of the game. DJ and EJ scored the first four points of the second half on dunks, tying the game while firing up the team, the crowd, and Chattanooga's bus. EJ was unstoppable in the second half as he scored 18 of his game-high 33 points, setting an IU record for most points by a freshman in his debut game.

Our defense improved enough to keep us from giving back the lead we eventually built. We started the season 1-0 with a 99-79 win. DJ scored 17 points, but only pulled down four rebounds. Sophomore guard, Armon Bassett scored 20 points and Crawford played like a human, only scoring 13 points on 4-7 shooting. I really thought he would shoot 91 percent every game that season. What a disappointment he turned out to be.

We were very good in stretches on offense, though even those stretches were more the result of having great athletes and very good shooters than of a well-run offense. If, as Knight said, the mental is to the physical as four is to one, then we were in trouble. Our physical had the potential to be very good. Our mental seemed to be pushing a door that had a pull sign on it.

One game into the season and our offense was to our defense as four is to one. We had trouble keeping the Chattanooga Mocs off the boards. We were outrebounded and we allowed them to pull down 10 offensive rebounds.

The game was well in hand at the 6:09 mark in the second half, when DJ committed a foul, and while he was up in the air, was undercut and came down hard, banging his head on the ground. He walked off the court, but the crimson to cream ratio on the floor had changed slightly as a result, giving us our first injury of the season. DJ suffered a slight concussion, but his injuries were not severe enough to keep him out of the Longwood game six days later.

We played Longwood and UNC Wilmington at home in the first round of the Chicago Invitational Tournament. Wins in those two games would put us in the semifinals in Hoffman Estates, Illinois. Longwood was in its first year as a Division I program and we had almost a full week to prepare for this game. It showed but not right away.

I guess I should have been happy in my search for consistency. Our defense continued to be bad. We continued to give up easy transition baskets and handle screens poorly. We also continued to start slowly. At the first TV timeout of the Longwood game we were down 8-7. By the time we reached the next TV timeout our athleticism had taken over and we were up by 10 points. We were still having defensive problems, but they were being disguised by our ability to score.

We continued to pull away. EJ continued to impress, and Crawford and Bassett continued to shoot a high percentage and contribute at a high level. DJ, however, had not been a presence on the boards yet this season. After two games he had a total of seven rebounds. We were performing in an impressively consistent way; bad defense, potent scoring.

We only allowed Longwood to score 49 points,[9] while we had six players score in double figures as we reached the century mark. The Samson Syllogism would hold that this was a good performance. It wasn't, but it was consistent.

If the Longwood and Chattanooga games are not enough to demonstrate this team's complete commitment to consistency, I present

[9] Which would have earned everyone in the stands free food at McDonald's if this were 1975.

exhibit three: IU versus UNC Wilmington. In what is undoubtedly the most maddening of the three, Wilmington started the game by setting a back screen for an alley-oop, hitting a three pointer, grabbing two offensive rebounds, and scoring on an uncontested put back in the first 90 seconds. In the two minutes following that opening salvo, they scored on three open layups, an open three-pointer, and two free throws.

After Stemler's uninspiring line as a starter against Chattanooga (0-2), zero points, zero rebounds, three fouls, Sampson decided to start DeAndre Thomas at the four spot. Thomas, who joined the Hoosiers with Jamarcus Ellis as junior college transfers from Chipola, arrived on campus weighing 356 lbs., according to Sampson at Hoosier Hysteria. By that night in October he was down to 298 lbs.

He got the start again against Wilmington, and decided to announce his presence with authority. DeAndre the Giant scored six of our first eight points. At the first TV timeout we were down 18-8, and less than thirty seconds later EJ picked up his second foul. We didn't get any points from a guard until the 12:51 mark.

EJ sat for less than two minutes in what I didn't know at the time was an act of great restraint for Sampson, before coming back in the game with two fouls. It was a coaching decision that bucked conventional wisdom, but in this case it worked out well. And since it worked out it was a good decision.

We once again relied on our superior athletic ability to overcome the early deficit we allowed to happen. This time, however, we didn't wait until the second half to assert ourselves. We tied the game at 24 with eight minutes to go in the half and then outscored Wilmington 28-8 in the final eight minutes. EJ finished the first half with 16 points, as did Bassett, which means, if my math is correct, that those two players scored 32

34

combined points in the last 12 minutes of the first half after not scoring at all for the first eight. The half-time score was 52-32.

The second half was another example of sloppy play, a large lead, and no repercussions. We had so much talent that a 95-71 outcome was far too close. EJ finished with 30 points. Bassett, who the announcers were fond of telling us had been completely overshadowed,[10] finished with 19 points. Crawford came off the bench strong again to score 15 points on 7-11 shooting, and DJ scored 12 points but only grabbed three rebounds, giving him 10 for the first three games of the season.

This team had built a very consistent profile. We completely reversed Knight's ratio. Our mental was to our physical as one is to four. We could score with ease, often without running any recognizable offense, but we turned the ball over too much. We were very bad in transition defense and help-side half court defense. We had real trouble defending the ball screen. We had trouble keeping smaller teams off the boards. And we gave up early leads, only to make that back with a spurt of decent defensive play coupled with a productive offensive stretch.

I had wild emotional swings watching them play. I found myself screaming in excitement when we had the ball, convinced that we were awesome and unstoppable because even with the sloppiness it was fun watching EJ, Bassett, Crawford, and DJ put it in the basket, only to be screaming and cursing less than a minute later when we were on the defensive end of the court. Under the best of circumstances during an IU game I have the emotional memory of an infant. This was far from the best of circumstances.

---

[10] In both the Longwood and the Wilmington games, two different announcers said, "Last year he was overshadowed by Mike Conley, Jr. And this year he's in danger of being overshadowed on his own team!"

This was more how Jerry[11] felt when George[12] lost his glasses. George, sans glasses, saw Jerry's girlfriend kissing his cousin, Jeffrey. Jerry was inclined to believe George because, even without his glasses, George was known to squint his way down to 20/30 vision.[13] Later, in Jerry's apartment, George glances across the room and says, "Hey, look, a dime!" and Jerry takes this latest show of superhuman eyesight as more evidence of his girlfriend's guilt until George goes to the fridge to grab an apple, reaches into the fridge and bites into a big, juicy onion. Jerry exclaims, "You're eating onions! You're spotting dimes! I don't know what the hell is going on!"

We were consistently frustrating, but we kept winning, so everything was just fine, right?

---

[11] Seinfeld

[12] Costanza

[13] There was an incident with raccoons that were really mailboxes.

Interlude Two: "What's That Say? Talk to the Audience? Argh, This is Always Death."

Sampson, blessedly, thankfully, while trying very hard to control the message, continued his tradition of providing information at press conferences that he didn't necessarily mean to provide. After the Chattanooga game Sampson met with the press to put a nice shine on that turd. "The story of that game is the second half."

In life there are things we want to be true and things that are actually true. Unfortunately for Sampson, the subject at the center of the story often wants the story to be one thing, but those writing the story see it as something completely different. As if to put the winky emoticon at the end of the sentence, Sampson's cell phone rang immediately after he told us what the story of the game was.

One half of outscoring our opponents didn't make that the story, no matter how much Sampson wished and told us that it was so. It was as though Sampson had seen something he really wanted in the Christmas display window;[14] a set of stories about this team's improvement. However, he wasn't confident in the ability of either the media or the fans to recognize this improvement on their own, so he was looking for more subtle and ingenious ways of planting the idea in their heads so they might think it was their own. He placed the advertisement of our improvement in the *Look* magazine of his postgame press conferences. It is best when one finds a theme on which to focus to begin dropping the seeds of that theme early and often.

"I thought tonight was a perfect game for this team," he said. "I couldn't have scripted it any better."

[14] A Red Rider 200 shot range-model air rifle?

Dear Michael Bay,

I am writing to recommend Kelvin Sampson as the screenwriter for your next big budget special effects extravaganza. I believe Kelvin would be the perfect fit for your style.

You have demonstrated throughout your career an ability to produce spectacle devoid of substance and plots devoid of sense (Armageddon, Transformers 1 and Transformers: Rise of the Fallen, Bad Boys I and II, and the video for Lionel Richie's "Do it to me.") Kelvin, through his admission that the Chattanooga game went better than he could have scripted has demonstrated a similar commitment.

Kelvin likes flash (see: everything Eric Gordon does on offense). He eschews almost anything that makes sense (see: allowing a 50-point first half by Chattanooga). He uses individual indicators as determinants (see: It was a good shot if it went in, or it was a good game if we won), as do you (see: There is suspense if there are explosions and special effects and a movie is good if the box office returns are good).

In short, Kelvin focus on style over substance and outcome over product make him the ideal candidate to pen your next explosigasmatron. Please feel free to contact me if you have any further questions.

Sincerely yours,

Jeff Taylor

Sampson continued to hint subtly in a "Flick said he saw a grizzly bear by Pulaski's candy store" kind of way, that everyone should write about how much we were improving and not how this was a team with great ability and poor play, or about phone calls.

"Our defensive is gonna come along," he said.

Look! I've written the theme you've been waiting for all your life! Listen to this sentence, "If you think back to our exhibition games, most of our bigs kept getting beat off the dribble, but it's two weeks later. This team is playing early like it should now and we're starting to get better."

Poetry! Sheer poetry, Kelvin! A+!

As a last ditch effort to get the story he wanted, Sampson found himself on Santa's lap with one chance left to make his case.

"They were slipping ball screens. We lay a blue piece of tape down the middle of the court at both ends, and we talk about the blue line. When you're away from the ball, when the ball's on the other side and your man's away from the ball, you've got to get to the blue line, and I know that one time they slipped the screen and we called a timeout 'cause Jordan was, you know, young guys have a tendency to play close to their man when the ball is away from them, instead of getting to a help-side…"

A weakness?

A weakness? Oh no, what was I doing? Wake up, stupid! WAKE UP!

"…but we'll get better at that. We're a lot better now than we were the last game, so the improvement is good to see."

But press conferences were not the only place Sampson had to try to steer the story toward our youth and improvement and away from cell phones and defensive problems. In a move in which the only foreseeable outcome was unforeseeable outcomes, Sampson began to do his weekly radio show live in front of an audience of students.

The Lords of Kobol were truly smiling upon us the day this decision was made as, like Sampson's press conferences, the radio show told us even more about him than he would have ever wanted and provided us insights he never intended.

Prior to the Wilmington game, *The I'm Contractually Obligated to Suffer Through This Once a Week, But I Can't Believe I Agreed to Do This In Front Of A Bunch Of Students Inside Indiana Basketball Coach's Show* debuted on radio stations across Indiana live from Foster Quad.

Previous Doctors had done shows like this in different ways, both on TV and radio, and almost all of them have been dreadful, Bob

Knight's version being the exception. Knight's shows demonstrated his sense of humor and disdain for these shows. He often used his radio show as a good time to catch up on mail or read the paper. And he used his television show to instruct and entertain. His shows were not a celebration of the great things on the court. They were a direct extension of his mood at the moment it was filmed. If he was angry, the show came off angry, if he was in a good mood, he joked and teased Chuck Marlowe. He once brought a jackass on the show so he could interview a Purdue fan. He leaned backwards and forwards in his chair making it impossible to keep him in the shot, he banged his microphone creating a horrible racket, and he took fan questions with the same respect he showed to reporters' questions, interchangeably. And the questions he got from Chuck Marlowe or Don Fischer had an equal chance of getting answered in a way that would satisfy the asker.

Everything about Sampson's version of this show showed his desire to control every aspect of the message. Knight never showed a desire to control the message. He *was* in control of the message. Everything about Sampson's answers showed his desire to avoid providing any real insight into the program, and his desire to be liked, by Fish, by the students in Foster Quad, and by the people listening on the radio.

The format of his version of the show was a short interview by Don Fischer, then questions from the live audience and callers. Sampson required that the students in attendance submit their questions in advance so he could choose the ones he wanted to answer. All the callers were screened, so you'd think this would provide ample protection against ass-basketry, but you would be wrong.

Sampson read a question from "my man Andre,"[15] who asked if

Sampson would be chest bumping EJ any more this season as he had done during one of the first two games. What you couldn't see on the radio was the mountain of white paper crumpled up around Andre, each page filled with a question that he either deemed uninteresting, unimportant, or too stupid to ask before inspiration struck and he put pen to paper with that gem.

The answer was yes.[16]

Another student asked a question about Sampson's statement from his first year about "sealing the border" as it pertains to recruiting. Instead of answering the question Sampson went full douche bag and flipped that shit. He asked the kid what he thought.

This kid would have needed more courage than most college students possess to tell Sampson the truth. What he was undoubtedly thinking was, *well, I think losing Tyler Zeller to North Carolina is a blow and it wouldn't have happened if you and your coaches knew how to follow the rules.* What the kid said instead was that he thought Sampson was doing a good job.

Sampson knew how that would play out and it was a cowardly thing to do to a kid who had the temerity to ask an honest question. He could, very easily, have shuffled that question to the bottom of the pile and not read it out loud. I'm sure there were more brilliant questions from Andre in there. Instead he put this kid on the spot to make himself look better.

While he wasn't able to use *The I'm Contractually Obligated to Suffer*

---

[15] Try to picture Bob Knight or Mike Davis referring to a student as "my man."

[16] They never chest bumped again. Sampson's man, Andre, must have felt so betrayed.

Through This Once a Week, But I Can't Believe I Agreed to Do This In Front Of A Bunch Of Students Inside Indiana Basketball Coach's Show to further his search for stories about the team's improvement, he was able to deflect attention from scandal and onto some lighter fare.

And with that, the topic of phone calls was shelved, at least for a while.

Interlude Three: Predictions? Pain

Predictions are easy. So easy, in fact that anyone can make them. They're made even easier by the fact that it doesn't matter if they're correct. They are completely meaningless but somehow entertaining. This is something ESPN realized years ago.

Of the radio programming on the ESPN network of stations your average hour is broken down as follows. :00-:08 Commercials (Tire Company) :08-:10 Payoff on the last hour's tease. :10-:15 Expert breaks down last night's story. :15-:19 Expert predicts something about tonight's contest. :19-:20 Tease some big story :20-:28 Commercials (Viagra) :28-:32 Read and respond to listener e-mail (most explaining why the host/the expert/nameless athlete who said something is a moron) :32-:38 Host predictions :38-:40 Tease some shocking story about how someone is a dope. :40-:48 Commercials (Debt Consolidation and Cialis) :48-:58 Expert who predicts something.

Unless it's Friday during football season, which looks like this :00-:08 Commercial (this weekend's football coverage and Tire Company) :08-:20 Expert who predicts the games. :20-:28 Commercials (this weekend's football coverage and Viagra) :28-:40 Expert predicts this weekend's games. :40-:48 Commercials (this weekend's football coverage, Debt Consolidation and Cialis) :48-:00 Expert predicts this weekend's games.

Unless it's a local afternoon drive time show. In that case the entire show is callers saying different versions of "The Colts are gonna win and here's why."

In short, it's experts making predictions, hosts making predictions and fans making predictions. All equally valid. All equally likely to be right. And the best part is that on Monday no one ever says, "Boy, I got that wrong over the weekend. There should be some consequences."

Of even more use, and requiring even more credentials, is to look back at something and tell people the things that anyone could have predicted, even though no one did.

There was a lot about our next two games in Chicago that anyone could have predicted. Our two opponents to conclude the Chicago Invitational Tournament in Hoffman Estates were Illinois State and Xavier. When you get further into a tournament and away from your home court the competition gets tougher. The combined record of our first three opponents was 4-5. The combined record for Illinois State and Xavier was 7-2.

Prior to the Wilmington game, Sampson said that they were the best team we had played so far. Prior to the Illinois State game, Sampson said *they* were the best team we had played so far. Prior to the Xavier game, he said *they* were the best team we had played so far. He wasn't wrong. The talent and skill level of each of these three opponents was better than any of the other teams we had played to that point. It was predictable that our competition would get tougher.

In our first three games we had shown a weakness on the boards. Against Chattanooga we were out-rebounded 34-32, allowing 10 offensive rebounds to the five we grabbed.[17] Wilmington out-rebounded us 28-25 and pulled down nine offensive rebounds to our four.

For a team with a coach who wanted rebounding to be a cornerstone of their identity, we were not a good rebounding team and fair or not, this seemed to be tied to DJ's lack of productivity on the glass: 10 total rebounds over those three games.

In Chicago, DJ totaled 17 rebounds in two games, posting his first double-double of the season. Consequently we out-rebounded both teams, but our turnaround was not complete. Illinois State pulled down 14 offensive rebounds and in the last six minutes of the Xavier game, when we needed to hit the glass the hardest, Xavier grabbed eight rebounds, while we had three. That DJ would finally begin playing to his capabilities was completely predictable, as were our continued struggles on the glass.

EJ's performance against Illinois State was exactly what we had come to expect from him. He posted 31 points in the game and 17 of our 30 total points in the first half. He scored every way available. He drove the lane and scored on layups and pull-ups. He hit open threes. He scored in transition and from the free throw line. His dominance against Illinois

---

[17] Against Longwood, a team we beat by 51 points, we did a better job on the glass, but we still allowed 11 offensive rebounds, a fact that is offset a little by Longwood"s 25 percent shooting, which provided them with 46 opportunities for offensive rebounds, of which they got around 25 percent. They had more offensive rebounds than we did, but we grabbed eight of out 17 misses. But none of that matters, as we beat by 51 points.

State was completely predictable.

But even great players have off nights. For EJ, an off night meant 4-12 from the field with three turnovers and four fouls. It also meant 12-12 from the line and a total of 20 points. It shouldn't have surprised anyone who watched EJ average 25.5 points over his first four games that an off night would mean he still led all scorers in the game.

We beat Illinois State by 13 points, extending our record to 4-0 and setting us up to play, say it with me, the best team we'd played so far, Xavier. Of all the things about this trip that were predictable, what should have surprised you like the sun rising every day is that our poor defensive play and our 1:4 ratio would catch up to us against a good team.

Sampson's policy of leaving players with two fouls in the first half was the first among the many things that caught up to us against Xavier. After moving Stemler to the bench and placing DeAndre the Giant in the starting lineup, the eighth wonder of the world slowly began to outstretch his role. He scored six of our first eight points against Wilmington and came out firing against ISU, taking three jump shots and one layup in the first two minutes, missing all of the jump shots. Determined to make up for that poor showing, he started the game against Xavier by firing and missing our opening salvo for the second game in a row, but his over-exuberance showed most against Xavier with his fouls. He committed his first foul going for the rebound of a DJ-missed free throw one minute into the game.

He picked up his second foul at the 16:21 mark in the first half on what has to be the worst way in the history of basketball to draw a foul. Xavier's C.J. Anderson gave a pump fake to get The Giant off his feet, which worked like a charm. And there was a moment, brief though it may have been, when Anderson felt a great sense of pride that all of the coaching he'd had and all the work he'd done on his pump fake had worked just the way he always hoped it would, a moment of knowing that all the hard work had been worth it, a brief second in that self-satisfied happy place we all go when everything just works. It was the same moment Wile E. Coyote had when he chased the roadrunner off the cliff just before he remembered there was gravity. Anderson was pushed right out of that happy place when all 300 lbs of The Giant came crashing down on his back. Crushing both Anderson's body and will to live. DeAndre didn't pick up his third in the first half, but Anderson was less than pleased with Sampson's decision to leave him in the game after his first foul.

With EJ it was a much different situation. EJ picked up his first foul five minutes into the game and his second foul at the 7:25 mark when we were down by four points. Sampson left him in the game and he picked up his third foul 14 seconds later, leaving him on the bench during Xavier's run and inhibiting him in the second half.

But it didn't end there. In fact it just got more confounding and less justifiable. DJ picked up his second foul with 1:16 left on the clock. For reasons unknown, Sampson left DJ in the game for the last minute of play, which worked great for 1:14, but DJ picked up his third foul with two seconds left in the half!

With DJ still on the court for that last 1:16, Xavier closed out the half with a run that put us behind by double digits. We started the second half with our two best players in foul trouble and we never got any closer than that.

When we got behind, what little offensive discipline we had disappeared. Our offense in the second half consisted entirely of drive, kick, three, and miss. Our 1-15 mark from the outside should have suggested a different strategy may have been needed, especially considering Sampson's stated position that if you take 30 threes and make 18 they are good shots, but making one of 15 means they were bad shots. Just as leaving EJ in with two fouls and having him pick up his third immediately might have suggested a reevaluation of that policy, but dance with the girl that brung ya seemed to be the order of the day, temporarily overriding the Sampson Syllogism.

That's not to say that there had been no effort or focus on making changes where they were needed. In previous press conferences, when he wasn't talking about our youth or how much we'd already improved, Sampson talked about our tendency to play too close to our man when he didn't have the ball. This type of play results in not having any defenders in position to help when their teammates get beat.

In meeting with the press after the game, Sampson spoke again about the work they do in practice by placing blue tape down the middle of the court, giving the players a visual representation of the help line. This is the standard method for teaching help-side defense and there was not a reporter in the room, or many fans outside the room, who were unfamiliar with the blue line down the center of the floor. There were, however, 14 basketball players in the locker room who, despite having been in these practices and seeing, if not tripping over the blue tape in the middle of the floor, didn't seem to know what the help line was.

Xavier and almost every opponent before them had been able to get great dribble penetration because we were out of position and nowhere near the help line. That our inability to play solid help defense would bite us in the ass eventually was predictable. Xavier was unranked and there weren't too many people who expected an IU loss, but knowing what we all should have known after watching those first four games, a loss to a quality, disciplined opponent was inevitable.

48

We were bound to lose a game eventually, especially with the fundamental issues we had exhibited thus far. We had a talented group of players who had yet to play a good game. Anyone who had just seen our box scores would have been shocked that we left Chicago with an 80-65 loss to an unranked Xavier team, but anyone who had watched could have predicted this.

One of Sampson's key terms was identity. He talked often since his arrival in Bloomington about the need for a team to develop an identity. The identity he wanted was a tough-minded team that played hard on defense and rebounded. Early in the season, with a team he never hesitated to remind us was young, it was crucial for a team to discover its identity.

This team might have already discovered theirs, and it wasn't a very good one. This was a team with great talent that was subject to long stretches of poor play, sloppy offense, slow and out of position defense, and bad transition defense, but good enough to put together a solid run of five to eight minutes each game that was likely going to be enough to get them a win. There was still a lot of time for this identity to change, but five games in and it was starting to take root.

Interlude Three: Well, Something's Not Right, Because Now I Can't See

The Xavier game provided us with the perfect example of what happens when you bring a knife to a gunfight. At the 17:01 mark in the first half Ellis fouled Derrick Brown as he threw down a dunk in transition. As Brown went to the free throw line, the officials noticed something was amiss. The power of the dunk had caused a portion of the net to become unhooked. What followed would be best described by kids today, or by someone trying to sound like kids today, as an EPICFAIL with multiple instances of FACEPALM.

The facilities manager came out with his ladder and we went to commercial. It was a bit early for the TV Timeout, but it was clear this was going to take a minute. Upon our return the net had gone from being out of one loop to hanging out of four or five of the loops on the rim. The facilities manager's plan of attack thus far was to try to force the net back through the loops with his keys, then with a switchblade, then consult with people on the ground, then give it another go with his keys, possibly a different key, then when the choice of keys was determined not to be the problem give the knife another go. Then, further consultation with the people surrounding the ladder, who were shouting helpful advice to him like, "Turn the middle side top-wise. Top-wise!"

As tough as it is for TV commentators to fill these kinds of gaps it's much tougher for the radio guys who can't even go to video highlights. Don Fischer and former Hoosier guard and future white-collar criminal, Todd Leary, gave it their best shot. They recapped the game to this point and gave a quick rundown of the box score.

It was then time to check in with the man on the ladder with keys and a switchblade who had gotten the net back through a number of the loops. WINNING! But he had skipped one in the process. FACEPALM. You can almost hear Fish shake his head at this point, but being the seasoned pro he is, he goes back to giving some analysis of the Burrell-Gordon match-up.

And then they decide to take the entire net down. FACEPALM

I've heard Leary's entire range of emotions on the air. He's been fired up at poor play, angry at the officials, and jubilant over victories. But I've never heard him as defeated as when they decided, after five minutes of working on the net, to just take the whole thing down and start from scratch.

Only Lando Calrissian knows what it's like to see a situation deteriorate this quickly. This deal kept getting worse all the time.

Having exhausted everything that could possibly be recapped from a game that was less than three-minutes old, the radio crew began listing things they could do to kill time. Fish suggested they send it back to the station to play music, but he realized that this wasn't 1985 and "nobody does that anymore."

"Joe could sing," offered Leary.

"Yeah, we could do that, too," agreed Fish, "but then we'd lose half our audience."

Fish then started naming the places nearby where they could go and buy a new net. The reporter doesn't normally want to become part of the story, but there didn't seem to be anyone there who could successfully change the net without help, so Fish was ready to step in with a "you buy, I'll fly" offer. But then he had an even better idea: They could finish eating the funnel cake he had sitting there. Theater of the mind.

There are purely visual things that work on the radio. Howard Stern has proven that over the course of his career, body waxing and naked women are prime examples of that phenomenon. No one had ever tried to broadcast a guy eating a funnel cake. Many of you are probably doubting the value of listening to Fish eat a funnel cake, but I'm telling you, it's gold, Jerry!

"Mmm-k, Tobb. I'b takemb, ma firsh bibe. Ss purby goo... Muh fought id woobee groaf by dow."

"It looks really good, Don. Can I have a bite?"

"NO! Mibe! Gedger owb."

"Fine. Sorry. Here's a napkin. You've got powdered sugar all over the place, Don."

"Leeemealome!"

In my mind, Fish gets very angry and protective of his funnel cakes.

On the TV side of the broadcast they went to commercial again. When they came back no progress had been made. There was still no net and there seemed to be a piece of plastic stuck in there that was causing a lot of difficulty. At least the guy hadn't gotten one of keys stuck in there.

Some people live their entire lives chasing greatness. Others have it thrust upon them in times of great turmoil. The guy who ran a new net across the court to the guy on the ladder saw his chance to be the hero to an arena full of people and millions more at home and he seized that moment. The reception he received from the grateful people was a wave of cheers that washed over him like a tsunami of love. He didn't stop to enjoy it, to feel their completely temporary and conditional love, he just went about the business of delivering that net. This kid was big time.

Twelve minutes into this fiasco, Joe Smith walked over to offer the guy on the ladder a screwdriver. He had been on a ladder, surrounded by craned-neck gawkers offering emotional support, if not any actual practical help, working on a net that was out of one hoop, then four, then off entirely with at first his own house keys, then a switchblade, and the thought that all of this could have been avoided if only the guy on the ladder had been in possession of a screwdriver, and that the only guy in the building who thought of this was part of the on-air talent for one of the teams playing and not one of the crane-necked gawkers is staggering. But I had seen nothing thus far to indicate that that level of ridiculousness was beyond the pale.

Either the screwdriver was not the answer to all their problems, or they were too proud to take Joe up on the only thing that could have stopped this farce, because they ignored Joe, who walked away, head hung low, but not before he, ever the helper and not one to let his pride prevent him from providing the solution, gave the screwdriver to Dakich. Joe Smith, you see, is not above knowing that it may not have been the screwdriver they were rejecting, but that there may be something about him personally that they just didn't like. In any event, the screwdriver turned out not to be the Deus Ex Machina, but they did take it from Dakich. And after the 15 longest minutes in sports history, a new net was hung and the two teams took to the court for another set of warm-ups.

Chapter Four: You Didn't Have to Get Into it, Baby

On October 25, 1997, I went to the movies with Bob Knight. We actually saw each other a couple of times that day. We met early in the day at his coaches clinic where he gave me his best wishes three different times and later that night we went on a double date to the movies.

We got there at separate times and he sat two rows behind me. He played it cool, not saying a word. After the movie, as we were walking across the parking lot, I wished him a happy birthday. He thanked me for my wishes and we went our separate ways. My girlfriend at the time was caught by surprise, as she didn't know it was his birthday, or that we were on a double date with Bob and Karen that night. In fact, I'm pretty sure she didn't know they were even in the theatre, but Coach and I shared a special day that I'm sure we both remember fondly.

We were there to see *The Edge*. If you haven't seen *The Edge*, let me fill you in on a few crucial details. And lest you feel that I am giving too much away, rest assured that I am only spoiling the movie about 10 minutes before David Mamet was going to do it anyway. In *The Edge,* Anthony Hopkins, Alec Baldwin, and Elle Macpherson head into the Alaskan wilderness so that Baldwin, the fashion photographer, can take pictures of Macpherson, who is married to Hopkins.

It's a wonderful movie if you hate being surprised. They land in Alaska and one of billionaire Charles Morse's (Hopkins) assistants says, "I took the liberty of speaking to the pilot and checking the engine log. Everything seems to be in good shape. I would not recommend you fly under any possibility of bird strike or ice." Morse quickly explains to photographer, Robert Green (Baldwin) that if we hit a flock of migrating birds "we're all dead."[18]

When they get on the plane Morse opens a copy of "Lost in the Wild" by D. Croyle with chapters like "Traps and Snares" and "Cleaning and Skinning Hides."

Upon arrival at their cabin, we are told, by Morse, that he retains all manner of facts, but he's not good at putting them to use. Then the keeper of the inn says, "We've got a problem with bears around here." And that "the Kodiak bear would just as soon kill you as look at you. And the one that's killed a man is a man-hunter the rest of his life. Nothing he'd rather eat than the taste of human flesh. A man-killin' machine."

Morse quids his pro quo by telling the innkeeper, who has lived in the wilderness his whole life, that you can make a compass out of a needle. The innkeeper gives his best, "I'll be damned. You'd think I would have known that, what with the fact that I have lived in the middle of nowhere Alaska my whole life, but don't that just beat all. I did *not* know

---

[18] The pilot was no Sully, clearly.

that" look.

Morse is not only intelligent, he's also jealous. He gives the stink-eye to both the inn keeper and the pilot who make mention that his wife, Macpherson, the model, who is there to have her picture taken for a magazine, is attractive.

They decide to take another short flight to find an old Indian for a picture as bad weather comes in. On the flight, Morse and Green discuss how Green also thinks Macpherson is hot. Morse turns to Green and says, "So, how are you going to kill me?" We don't even get a chance to even say, huh? Because guess what happens.

If you guessed bird strike, award yourself one Coke. They run into a bird strike and their plane crashes. Morse, Green, and Steve the Redshirt survive, but the handy survival book floats ominously to the bottom of the lake. If it weren't for that warning at the beginning about how dangerous bird strikes can be, we would have never understood why the plane crashed after it flew into that flock of birds.

The fact that Morse told the innkeeper, and all of us, that you can make a compass out of a needle sure was handy. Now they can use a needle to make a compass and walk back toward civilization. A shiny bobbin for anyone who can guess what happens next. Remember the prophetic words of the innkeeper, from just before he learned about the needle compass deal. That's right. They run into a bear. They escape the bear this time, but Steve the Redshirt cuts himself pretty bad and the bear shows up to eat him. If only we'd been given some information about what happens after a Kodiak bear tastes human flesh. You can imagine where it goes from here.

"He fixes the cable?"

"Don't be fatuous, Jeffrey."

I don't even remember how it ends, but I can always go to 15 minutes before the credits to find out.

The only thing David Mamet didn't tell us 15 minutes before it happened was that I was going to wish Bob Knight a happy birthday on the way through the parking lot

Telling you in advance what's going to happen isn't the only way to fail at misdirection. Let's say your wife or girlfriend asks you what you were thinking and you just happened to be having nasty, filthy, dirty thoughts about her best friend. There are three possible answers:

A.) I was thinking about doing filthy, nasty, things with your best friend;

B.) I was ABSOLUTELY NOT thinking about doing filthy, nasty, possibly illegal, certainly immoral and definitely not approved of by you, acts with your best friend. Why do you ask? Quit looking at me like that! Why don't you trust me?!;

C.) Nothing. What do you want to do for dinner?

Before choosing the correct answer, we should probably examine the outcome you hope to achieve with said answer. For example, if you were hoping to work this into some kind of double-trouble mix-in kind of deal, your only hope is answer "A." But that presupposes that you and your old lady live "the lifestyle."

If you don't live in a 1970s let's all go to a key party world, the best outcomes you could hope for would be to avoid any kind of trouble and to get to eat dinner.

If either of those is your endgame then "A" is not for you. It almost guarantees you the exact opposite, plus the one person who is contractually obligated to have sex with you won't. "B" also gets you nowhere. I think this is exactly what Shakespeare was talking about when he wrote, "defensive much?"[19] So, "C" is really your only choice. She had no way of knowing you were up to the devil's business without you blathering on about it, and she probably assumed you were thinking about food anyway.

Sampson, apparently in preparation for that job interview with Michael Bay, called David Mamet for tips on audience misdirection. Mamet is far from a one trick pony. He's not locked in to the misdirection by telling people exactly what's going to happen 15 minutes before it happens method. He gave Sampson the equally effective, say explicitly, repetitively, that you are going to do one thing. Say it with such force and conviction, and back it up with all the reasons why you are going to do that, then you do exactly the opposite 10 minutes later, and not only will no one see it coming, but they'll also see what a brilliant gambit it was to promote with such vehemence a complete lie. And further, they'll see why it was necessary for you to go to all the trouble of bringing it up in the first place. In other words, "Answer B," which Sampson used with dogged persistence.

And he used *The I'm Contractually Obligated to Suffer Through This Once a Week, But I Can't Believe I Agreed to Do This In Front Of A Bunch Of Students Inside Indiana Basketball Coach's Show* and *Coaches Report* on the pre-game radio show as the platforms to launch his campaign to explicitly deny things that don't need denial.

---

[19] I think that's in King Lear.

The inverse relationship that existed between his answers and what he ended up doing made it seem as though no other approach ever occurred to him. The more detail he went into to justify his decision, the further from that decision his action ended up being.

Fish must have noticed our awful defensive play, or just listened to Sampson talk about how ~~bad our help-side~~ much we've improved in our help-side defense, because he asked Sampson about playing a zone during the *The I'm Contractually Obligated to Suffer Through This Once a Week, But I Can't Believe I Agreed to Do This In Front Of A Bunch Of Students Inside Indiana Basketball Coach's Show*. Sampson said, "We haven't practiced zone enough to put it into play. I'm not sure we've gone over it more than once." Fish tried to move on to another topic, but Sampson kept coming back to it. He (didn't really) say, "I hate zone defense. What's zone defense? I *am* playing a zone defense? Get outta the road," which was a pretty strong, if not always on topic denial.

Our man-to-man defense was no better against Georgia Tech than it was against Xavier. We gave up easy baskets and weren't boxing out. At the under eight minute TV Timeout in the first half we were down 29-25. If only we'd been working on a zone enough to deploy it in a circumstance such as this one. Drats!

We came out of that timeout and went right into a zone. And it worked. After switching to the zone, Georgia Tech went almost seven minutes without scoring and our four-point deficit became a four-point lead at the half. We finished the game with 37 rebounds to their 32 and played them even in the second half to come away with an 83-79 win.

During the same show, when Fish asked Sampson about available minutes he went into a long, loocooooooong explanation about how many minutes are available between the four and five spots per game (80) and how "DJ gets 30, DeAndre gets 20, Lance gets 25 or so, and the rest go to Eli. So we have to redshirt Mike White." He (didn't really) continue "There's really no other option. I wish you'd quit attacking me like this. It's really unprofessional and makes you look like a douche. Man, Fish, I thought you were better than that. Why did YOU decide to redshirt Mike White? Hmm? Yeah, I thought so. You ain't so bad, now, are you? Tough guy. Let's take some more phone calls so I can talk about the weather with some guy in Terre Haute."[20]

Mike White entered the game at the 14:13 mark in the first half. The necessity of redshirting White didn't even have the staying power of our inability to play zone. With so few minutes to distribute to so many players it was truly amazing that there were 20 minutes to give to this other, non-DJ, White. He played well and provided some spark off the bench. He had to work off some rust but at least for this one game, pulling the redshirt off White was a good move.

The Coaches Report, during the pre-game show is usually recorded about 50 minutes prior to the tip, right after Fish does the live intro. When Fish asked Sampson the standard starting line question during that Coaches Report he said, "DJ, DeAndre, Eric, Tone, and Jordan." And (didn't really) follow that up with, "Absolutely 100 percent Jordan. You know, he's a great kid. I can't envision him doing anything wrong. I actually find it kind of insulting to me, to Jordan and especially to his wonderful parents that you would ever hint that he might do something less than saintly someday. "

Sometime in the 40 or so minutes after he finished telling Fish the

---

[20] That last part happened. The call screener let a guy through who engaged Sampson in a conversation about the weather. No joke to make there. That's just the kind of show this was.

starting line up, Sampson announced that Crawford was suspended for three games for violating unspecified team rules and for threatening to dunk on Lebron James at a skills camp in two years. I don't know what he did, aside from the Lebron thing, but coaches don't normally just go around suspending people for no good reason, so I had to assume Crawford screwed the pooch in some typical 18-year-old way.

Based on how true Sampson's statements turned out to be, I'm sure glad he didn't say, while suspending Crawford, "that's the end of our discipline problems and that Crawford's suspension should be the wakeup call these guys need to know how important following the rules and doing things the right way is to me and my staff." I have this feeling that wouldn't have ended well.

The length of Crawford's suspension was exactly the number of games we had leading up to the Kentucky game and we won all three, including a trip to Southern Illinois to play a true road test against what many expected to be a tough opponent. That three game stretch proved Sampson's decisions right.

Mike White's play over the course of those three games justified his activation. He was rusty, but active against Georgia Tech, Southern Illinois, and Tennessee State. He went from being redshirted to playing the most minutes off the bench in each of those three games.

After making the switch to zone against Georgia Tech, we played a considerable amount of it over these three games. And it was effective. We looked better defensively in the zone than we had all year in the man-to-man, and maybe Crawford learned a lesson.

I couldn't come up with any reason that made sense why Sampson would go on the radio and expound on the reasons why he was going to do something and then do the exact opposite. Either he believed each of those things he was saying and was caught off guard by the need to play Mike White, go to a zone, or suspend Crawford, or he had an idea that each of those things was possible, but figured that the best way to address each of these questions was to say unequivocally that they were not going to happen.

So why go into a long discourse on available post minutes if you thought there was a chance that Mike White would need to play? What's to gain by going on and on about it? Why not just say it still hasn't been decided? We wouldn't know any different. Why say you've never even practiced zone if you knew you might use it in the next game? Why not just say that it's something we've practiced, but aren't likely to use? Or we think man-to-man is our best chance to win, but if we feel the need to change it up, we will? I believe it's possible he didn't know about Crawford when he announced the line up, but that segment is recorded less than an hour prior to the tip, which means he either suspended Crawford and lied about the line up or suspended him 20 minutes prior to the start of the game and that information didn't get relayed to the broadcast team prior to tip-off.

The combination of the three is either a big coincidence that just happened to make it look like Sampson either doesn't know what's going on in his own program or that he intentionally mislead people for no good reason.

I'll let you be the judge, but neither answer makes him look very good.

The fact that the coach is that disconnected with the reality of his team or that he felt the need to go on the radio and say things that weren't true for no discernible reason is baffling. It makes one wonder about the mindset of someone who would lie just to lie, when there's nothing to gain by it. How likely is he to lie when there is something at stake?

Thankfully, we'd probably never have to find out.[21]

There were other things of interest to come out of these three games besides victories and odd mistruths, the first being Sampson's decision to play people in the first half with two fouls.

EJ picked up his first foul less than a minute into the Tennessee State game and his second foul at the 12:57 mark. Instead of sitting him for the half while we had a 14-4 lead, he rested him for a few minutes and then put him back in the game. At the 6:12 mark, with a 34-17 lead, EJ got caught up in the air near the free throw line and came down hard on his back. He came out of the game almost immediately and did not return.

Sampson's decision to put EJ back in the game with two fouls was certainly consistent with his previous decisions, but it continued to be a bad idea. I had hoped that after EJ picked up his third foul in the first half against Xavier and had to sit while they went on the run that pushed the game out of reach, and after DJ picked up his third foul with two seconds to go in the half, that Sampson would have re-evaluated that position, but he did not and three games later it ended up putting our best player on the bench for what could have been multiple games.

DJ continued to play better and better after his performance in the Xavier game. He posted a double-double in each of the three games and when EJ went down against Tennessee State, DJ came up huge. He scored a career-high 29 points on 11-15 shooting and grabbed 13 rebounds in what was by far his best game of the season to date. If there

---

[21] Crap. Did I just jinx us?

was one positive to come out of EJ's injury it was that DJ cemented his position as the leader of this team. If the Xavier game was DJ getting Nikki's phone number at the bar, the Tennessee State game was him dancing with Lorraine. After the Tennessee State game he was all growns up.

Interlude Four: Talking Points

"Governor Palin, address your position on global warming and whether you think it's manmade or not."

"Gwen, we don't know if this climate change whoosey-whatsit is manmade or if it's just a natural part of the end of days. But I'm not gonna talk about that. I wanna talk about taxes. Because with Barrack Obama you're gonna be payin' higher taxes. But not with me and my fellow maverick. We are not afraid to get maverick-y in there and ruffle feathers. And not got to allow that. And also, too, the great Ronald Reagan."

When I listened to Sampson's postgame press conferences I didn't feel like I was listening to a politician take whatever question was asked, ignore it, and go right to their talking points. It was more preposterous than that. I felt like I was listening to Tina Fey spoofing Sarah Palin sticking to her talking points.

Sampson had an amazing ability to stick to what he wanted to talk about. We'd seen it all season. He was very fond, right from jump street, of telling us how young this team was and of pointing out how much we'd improved. After the Tennessee State game, in which DJ scored 29 points and grabbed 13 rebounds, Sampson wanted to talk about our guards and how we didn't have very many of them, what with Crawford being suspended and EJ going out in the first half after getting hurt when he should have been on the bench with his second foul.

The second question, after the obligatory "How's your star player who must to have been hurt pretty badly to not even come back out to the bench in the second half?"[22] was about how DJ played. Sampson said:

"We were going to DJ as much as we could. I think DJ had 33 touches tonight. Sometimes people confuse shot attempts with how many times they get the ball. There are some times DJ may get the ball 30 times and only have seven shot attempts 'cuz they double him every time he touches it. But he had 34 touches tonight and he had, I think, 24 shot attempts. Of course when you get fouled, just so we all know, that's a shot attempt that doesn't get recorded as a shot attempt. It's a free throw attempt, not a shot attempt. But, I thought our kids did a good job getting the ball to him. And even the five shots he missed were open looks. And I think DJ's starting to take pride in this double-double thing, too. One of the special things we do with our team is signing that bubble and Jamarcus and DJ both have been signing it quite a bit lately. But DJ's a senior. He's gotten better every game he's played."

OK. So far, so good. That was a long answer that wandered into the rules on recorded shot attempts, but it was on topic. And he seemed ready to go on about DJ for another minute or so, but then he remembered his talking points.

"When EJ went down, and even if he could have come back I wouldn't have brought him back. Our guards have obviously been playing too many minutes. Nothing we can do about that. We were one foul away from playing four post guys there at the end." And then he followed it up with "We have five guards. Right now I only see two of them."

Sampson knew he had to hammer home the point that we were playing short of guards so he interjected it into other people's responses as well. When DJ was asked about a three pointer he took as the shot clock expired late in the game, Sampson piped in, "Five more minutes and he'd have been the point guard."

---

[22] Sampson's response: "Yeah, he'll be fine."

Sampson was asked about the run Tennessee State made in the second half that cut the lead to seven before Stemler hit back to back threes he said:

We got a little sloppy, um, ball handling, um, sometimes, we just had odd line ups out there ... Armon probably needed some rest ... Sometimes kids make mental errors, fatigue errors. You could tell. We were worried about it. There's nothin' we could do about it. We didn't have a substitute. When I made the decision to discipline Jordan, um, we knew these three games were going to be tough. I'm just glad, I'm really happy we're 3-0. I mean, we won all three games. That's the most important thing to me. I mean, I'm not really into analyzing this game. We won it. A month from now it's gonna be a W, just like the Southern Illinois game is a W. No different.[23] We get EJ back and Jordan back. Both of them will be back this week. That'll make Armon and Tone (a nickname Sampson used for Jamarcus Ellis frequently in press conferences) a lot better players.

He was asked about how much the team had practiced against the press and whether having EJ in there would have made it easier to handle, he said, "With Jordan in there it would be easier. It's another guard." He clearly wanted to talk about our lack of guards in this game. Ask him anything and he brought it back to the guards.

And then he was asked a question he should have been able to answer in his sleep, and if the time spent thinking about the team's identity was proportionate to the importance he claimed to place on it, this one should have been a no brainer, but so focused was he on talking about our guards and how we didn't have enough of them, he vapor-

---

[23] Oh, and let's not forget the need to work in the Sampson Syllogism. Damn, he's a pro with those talking points.

locked a bit and slammed a hard right into one of his talking point answers. He was asked, "What is this team's identity right now?" He didn't have my answer about their identity handy, as I hadn't written it yet, so he went with the "And also, too, the Great Ronald Reagan," answer.

I thought we played. I couldn't have asked for a better 17 minutes to start the game.[24] Our defense was outstanding, and give that kid [Tennessee State's, Price who scored 34 points] some credit now.[25] You say, who was guarding him? Armon, the first half, you know, he hit a three at the buzzer. We would have been up 16. You take a couple of those threes away and we probably would have been up 20 at half time and that was a good first half.[26] I worry a little bit about the second half, especially when EJ went down,[27] but I think we're getting better in every area.[28] Our rebounding is better. Our defense is better. I thought we ran our stuff really good the first half, executing. When Lance and Mike and DJ are playing a majority of the minutes together, offensively, we just spread the floor and let Tone and Armon get in the gaps. We attempted 36 free throws, so we're getting good in a lot of different areas. I'm pleased with our progress."

Remember, that was a question about the team's identity, not "Kelvin, your vast improvement, please show it to us" or "Which parts of the games would you like to focus on to the exclusion of other parts of the game?"

If that long, rambling mess of an answer accurately reflected his understanding of this team's identity, then Agent Kujan had a better idea about the identity of Keyser Soze when he and Verbal Kint were having their little chat. The only thing it accurately reflected was Sampson's belief in the power of the talking point. Stay on target. Stay on target.

Chapter Five: Two Great Hates to Hate Great Together

The thousand injuries of Billy Packer I had borne the best I could, but when he ventured upon inventing statistics to back up his point, I vowed revenge. I have felt personally wronged by Billy Packer many times, but never as much as in his March 26, 2007, appearance on *Costas Now*, where he was scheduled to be the foil to the great Myles Brand.

Billy, while making the point that many student-athletes would not

---

[24] Step 1: Focus on a small segment of the game.

[25] Step 2: Compliment the opponent, for whom we have great respect.

[26] Step 3: Tell people what might have been if the whole of reality was different.

[27] Step 4: Remind people we didn't have all of our guards

[28] Step 5: Let's talk about the positives

have been accepted to their schools had it not been for their athletic ability said, "I don't know how many of them wouldn't get in. Let's just make up a percentage. Ten to 15 percent of these kids would get in."

With those kinds of numbers to back up your position it becomes pretty unassailable. The numbers don't lie; 85 to 90 percent of all student-athletes don't have the grades to get into school without sports.

But, wha, wait … did he just say, "let's make up a percentage?"

Let's face it, people believe 75 percent of what they hear on TV to begin with, and when you add statistics to those statements that number jumps to 89 percent. Using the Packer Method to create statistics to give yourself that bump is just not fair. They've done studies. Sixty percent of the time, it works every time.

This was the tipping point for me.

The tipping point wasn't earlier that month when Billy suggested that Charlie Rose would just "fag out" on him if Billy got him a gig as a runner for the Final Four, or the next month when Ohio State center and star of HBO's *Hung*, Greg Oden, was called for traveling in the post and Packer said, "Travel, but a pretty good move." It wasn't even when he hired a psychic to find the murder weapon in the O.J. Simpson trial, or when he took the psychic and his sons in disguise to do a "thorough search" of the area for the weapon.[29] Nor was it in 2006 when he slammed the NCAA Selection Committee for including so many mid-major teams, which was the year that George Mason made an improbable run to the Final Four. Seldom right and wrong again, Billy.

He's said repeatedly that he's "often wrong, but never in doubt."
[29] That's not made up. He really did that.

To be so sure of your own stance, even when you know it's wrong, is a strange position to take in life, but as someone who's also pretty sure of his position most times I can't hate him too much for that. But the Packer Method is offensive. It smells like pure gasoline.

My dislike for Billy Packer and his "method" is matched only by my hatred for the University of Kentucky. We learn our sports loyalties at early ages. That's when we attach the most meaning to those teams, when they become a large part of how we identify ourselves. It's also when we learn about rivalries.

In Clarksville in the 1970s and 1980s you had a choice. You could place yourself into one of three categories, based purely on stereotypes. You could choose to be ghetto and enjoy an incredibly sloppy style of basketball that consisted of a lot a fast breaks and turnovers by choosing to be a fan of Denny Crum's Louisville Cardinals. You could choose to a complete redneck who has a hard time choosing between his can of Skoal and his semi-attractive cousin and be a Kentucky fan. Or you could be one of the chosen. You could embrace goodness and light. You could choose hard-nosed man-to-man defense and motion offense and be a Hoosier fan.

I chose well, but this choice was not entirely my own. I had a great deal of help from my family. My parents were kind of noncommittal. They were more or less willing to root for any of the local teams. Thankfully, I had cousins who would show me the right way to live.

It was always great fun to argue with kids at school and in my neighborhood about whose team was better. And we all had our arguments. The University of Louisville won two NCAA titles, one in 1980, and one in 1986. The University of Kentucky had five national championships. IU was in the midst of a golden era, with three NCAA titles and six Big Ten Championships in 12 years.

But it runs deeper than rivalry for me.

By the time Bob Knight took over as head coach in 1971, Indiana and Kentucky had played 11 times, but only twice since the end of World War II. An annual series was started in the 1970-1971 season that has continued, uninterrupted, to this day.

The 1972 season was Knight's first and legendary Kentucky coach, Adolph Rupp's last. Rupp was forced to resign at the end of the season, having reached the mandatory retirement age of 70. Rupp, having been born in 1901 had reached his lifetime goal of becoming the second most famous Adolph in world history. Because the guy in first place pretty much ruined that name for the rest of time, Rupp is assured of maintaining his second place status in perpetuity. So he's got that going for him, which is nice.

In December 1971, Indiana had not beaten Kentucky in their last five meetings, a drought lasting just under 30 years.[30] Those five consecutive losses by IU followed a perfect 6-0 record for the Hoosiers against the Wildcats dating back to their first meeting in December 1924 when we kicked their asses 20-18.

This has been a series of streaks, first the 6-0 streak by IU to start the series, followed by Rupp's 5-0 mark, then Knight's 5-0 start. Kentucky countered by winning nine of the next 13 matchups. Indiana then went 4-1 in the next five. Two of the next three went to UK, followed by a 5-0 stretch by the Wildcats that was ended by an IU win, followed by another 5-0 run by UK. The most recent two matches had been a 1-1 split.

[30] Our last win was in December 1942, which was 10 years into Rupp's UK tenure and just over three years into Adolph #1's tenure in Poland.

Many of the games had been extremely close. Since the annual tilts began in 1970, 12 games have been decided by one basket (four in the 70s, three in the 80s, and five in the 90s). Also, there have been a number of lopsided games with 14 decided by double digits, with one of each occurring in the 1975 season.

In our regular season matchup in December 1974 we easily handled Kentucky, beating them 98-74. We outplayed them on both ends of the floor and had Knight not pulled the starters from the floor with over eight minutes to play, the margin of victory would likely have been much greater. Fast forward to March 1975 and a rematch in the Final Four, this time with IU star Scott May just returning to play after breaking his arm in the last week of the season. Kentucky ended our perfect season 92-90. Had it not been for May's injury there was no way Indiana would not have easily dispatched them again and beaten Coach Wooden and UCLA for what ended up being his final title.

So, yes, the reasons for my hatred of UK predate my own existence by roughly nine months. It's quite possible I was conceived in rage following this loss.[31]

The 1975 injustice was not the only time we met in the NCAA tournament. We met in 1973 and again in 1983. We bested them in 1973, but bowed to them in 1983 in the second round, putting an end to a great season in another reversal of an earlier decision.

Part of what has made this rivalry so intense is the overall quality of the teams. In 10 of our meetings IU has come into the game ranked in the top five. The same can be said 12 times of UK. Six times we've met with both teams in the top five, and six times one of the two teams was ranked

[31] I cannot confirm or disconfirm this supposition as I am unwilling to broach the subject with my parents. It gives me the willies to even think about it.

first at tip off, with each team scoring a win over the number one team in the land once. In contrast there have only been three times when both teams have entered unranked.

And if it stopped there, with close games, high-stakes match-ups, winning and losing streaks, and geographic proximity, it would just be a great rival and a team I would enjoy watching us beat. In short, UK would be Purdue, a team I'd much rather beat than lose to, but not a team for which I can muster any amount of animus.

With Kentucky it's more, and with good reason. It's more because of Kentucky's history of cheating and a decades-long acceptance of these practices. Not only is Kentucky a rival, but they represent everything I abhor.

Much of what follows I owe to the work Todd Gould did in his book *Pioneers of the Hardwood: Indiana and the Birth of Professional Basketball.*

UK won their first three national championships in 1948, 1949, and 1951, all for Adolph Rupp, already well into his second decade as UK head coach. Kentucky fans are quick to point out the greatness of Rupp and their tradition of winning. They do, after all, lay claim to seven NCAA championships. What they aren't so quick to point out is Kentucky's role in the largest gambling scandal in college basketball history.

Before any Kentucky player agreed to take a dime from bookies to shave points in games they had already become accustomed to taking money. Rupp was known to motivate with the stick; he yelled and screamed and berated his players, standard college coaching tactics, in other words, but he also used the carrot. As Charles Rosen puts in his book *Scandals of '51*, "Rupp's boys regularly received cash from either Rupp himself, or from 'Boosters.' The sums ranged from $10 to $50, depending on how well the players performed."[32]

Rupp's team of paid amateur athletes won the NCAA title in 1948, many of whom took their special definition of "amateur status" to London for the 1948 Olympics, where they brought home the gold.

Upon their return, a local liquor distributor told Alex Groza, University of Kentucky and Olympic standout that he could expect $50 a month until he graduated.

Midway through the 1948-1949 season, former UK football player and local boy done good, Nick "The Greek" Englisis paid a visit to UK star senior Ralph Beard's hotel room following a game at Madison Square Garden. He greeted him in the manner all UK players had grown accustomed; he told him he played a great game and gave him money.

Englisis and his partners pursued Beard and his teammates Alex Groza and Dale Barnstable, offering them money to push the margin of victory up past the point spread. Each player accepted $100 to beat the spread against St. John's. They also took $100 each to beat up on DePaul and Vanderbilt in January 1949.

Then, in February they agreed to hold a game against Tennessee under the spread. They were paid $500 each for their efforts. Kentucky rolled into the NIT as the number one seed where they were paired with Loyola Chicago in the first round. Their attempt to shave points backfired on them as they shaved too many and lost to Loyola by 11 in a huge upset.

Beard and Groza graduated in 1949, but Barnstable was still around, as were the bookies, so Beard and Groza were replaced by Walter

[32] In 2007 dollars this is was roughly $37,000.

Hirsch and Jim Line as the fixers du jour. And the price went up. Instead of getting payouts of $100 a game these three were now making $500 to $1,000 per fix.

This went on unabated through the 1951 championship season with UK center Bill Spivey becoming involved in the game fixing activities. After an early season loss, Rupp gave each of his players $50 to keep them happy, as they had a long season ahead. He claimed that the money was "left over from a fund used to send the UK players to the London Olympics," three years previous.

On July 25, 1951, players from Bradley University were arrested for their role in point shaving and ratted on the Kentucky players. On October 19 of the same year, Beard and Groza, then players and owners of the new NBA franchise the Indianapolis Olympians, were arrested. The next day Dale Barnstable was also brought in. They sang like canaries, see.

In January 1952, Bill Spivey voluntarily resigned from UK basketball because of suspicions that he had been fixing games. In February, Jim Line and Walter Hirsh were arrested and flipped on Spivey, who admitted to the *Louisville Courier-Journal* that he had been approached about dumping games, but denied ever doing it. In court, Spivey denied ever having been approached. He was indicted on perjury charges in late March.

Before Spivey ever came to trial the UK athletic board found that he was part of a conspiracy to fix Kentucky basketball games during the 1950-1951 season and as a result, he was banned from playing for Kentucky ever again.

The next day Judge Saul Streit handed down his verdict on Beard, Groza, and Barnstable. They each received suspended sentences and indefinite probation. In his ruling, Streit said that he had taken statements from former players and various UK officials.

"I found undeniable evidence of athletes, cribbing on examinations, illegal recruiting, a reckless disregard for the players' physical welfare, matriculation of unqualified students, demoralization of athletes by the coach, the alumni and the townspeople."

The point shaving scandal of 1951 almost destroyed college basketball. It involved players from City College of New York, Manhattan College, and Bradley as well as UK. All of this must have completely shocked Coach Rupp, who was "often seen in the company of known gamblers in Lexington."[33] He boasted to reporters in April 1951 "Gentlemen, I'll guarantee you this: Gamblers couldn't touch my boys with a 10-foot pole."

Rupp responded to Streit's condemnation by saying "Ahh it's not *that* bad. The Chicago Black Sox threw games. But these kids only shaved points. College teams go to New York and find odds for the basketball games in the newspapers. If we allow newspapers to print odds for guttersnipes who infest the sport, I think it's time we checked up on some of the newspapers. Why condemn kids for one mistake in a lifetime? Let's be more lenient toward them."

UK President Herman Lee Donovan and Kentucky governor Lawrence Wetherby defended the university and blamed "radio stations, newspapers, magazines and college administrators and coaches throughout the land.'" In other words, everyone but Rupp and his players, which is an attitude that has served UK fans well for decades. Be more lenient toward our players and coaches who cheat. It's clearly someone

[33] Which must have been hard to avoid as the entire state is built on three things: tobacco, bourbon, and horse racing.

else's fault. Let's blame, um…newspapers! Yeah, it's the newspaper's fault for printing the odds or running the story. They're jealous and out to get us!

On August 11, 1952, the SEC barred UK from playing conference games for one year and demanded Rupp be removed, but the university refused to remove him saying, "We still believe Adolph Rupp to be an honorable man. We also feel the punishment we have received is excessive for the violations which we have been charged and to which we have confessed, violations which also have been committed by other members of the SEC in recent years."

See, not only was it not their fault, but everyone was being too hard on them and besides, everyone else was doing it.

The NCAA shut down the entire Kentucky basketball program for the 1952-1953 season finding that they had been "in violation of NCAA rules and regulations on two counts, in that athletes received pay for participation in athletics" and "athletes were certified as eligible for NCAA events when ineligible."

Rupp was never reprimanded for running a dirty program and continued to coach and win, never making any concession that what he had been doing was wrong or abnormal.

Rupp took his teams to two more Final Fours, winning in 1958 against Seattle University and losing in 1966 to Texas Western in one of the most important games in NCAA history. Texas Western was the first team to play for a national championship with a starting five comprised of all black players. At the height of the Civil Rights Movement Rupp's Runts, so named because their tallest starter was 6'5 Tommy Kron, were comprised of other starters Thad Jaracz, Larry Conley, Louie Dampier, and future Hall of Fame NBA coach Pat Riley, as well as reserves Cliff Berger, Bob Tallent, Steve Clevenger, Brad Bounds, Jim LeMasters, Gene Stewart, Tommy Porter, Bob Windsor, Gary Gamble, and Larry Lentz, all of whom were white.

In a game with the cultural significance of Ali-Frasier I and the 1980 U.S. Olympic hockey game this wasn't just a battle between two good basketball teams. Kentucky, their coach, and their fans were on the wrong side of humanity. In a game charged with racial tension, at a time when fire hoses were being turned on black protestors and black churches were being bombed, Rupp used racial epithets at halftime to help motivate his team telling them, according to *Sports Illustrated* reporter Frank DeFord, who was present in the locker room, "You've got to beat those coons" and that Thad Jaracz "go after that big coon."

After the defeat Rupp spent the next three years in defiance of UK president Dr. John Oswald's directive that Rupp integrate the basketball program, as the rest of the university had been integrated. Rupp was vocal in his opposition, as assistant coach Harry Lancaster tells it in his book *Adolph Rupp As I Knew Him,* "That son of a bitch is ordering me to get some niggers in here. What am I going to do? He's the boss."

Rupp eventually relented, signing 7'2 center Tom Payne in 1969, proving once and for all that he wasn't a racist because he had at least one black friend.

Rupp's successor, Joe B. Hall, had some success of his own, winning the 1978 national championship and, as Jackie MacMullan describes in *When The Game Was Ours,* promptly placing his five starters on the team for the World Invitational Tournament. He started his five guys for each game of the tournament over little-used bench players Earvin Johnson and Larry Bird.

But, like the 1948, 1949, and 1951 championships, the 1978 championship was tainted. That title was won while UK was under NCAA penalties for providing gifts and incentives to recruits that were imposed in 1976. As part of these sanctions 12 boosters, whose names were not released to the public, were forbidden from having any more contact with the basketball program.

Hall was a man with long ties to UK basketball. He was a player on the 1949 championship team, playing alongside Ralph Beard, Alex Groza, and Dale Barnstable, where he learned all he needed to know about how things were done at UK. Hall retired from coaching in March 1985, shortly after his team's final game in the NCAA tournament that year, citing his age, 56, as the primary factor, and not a moment too soon as he was only 14 years away from the mandatory retirement age that forced Rupp to leave kicking and screaming in 1972. Eddie Sutton was hired as his replacement and looked to continue UK's fine tradition of putting winning above all other considerations.

But before Sutton could get to the business of winning and cheating there was a small matter of all the cheating that Hall had been doing. In October 1985 two reporters for the *Lexington Herald-Leader*, Jeffrey Marx and Michael York, published a series of articles uncovering what has to be the most confounding case of sustained cheating, its reporting and its consequences in the history of athletics. A careful reading of the events surrounding the Joe B. Hall tenure raises a number of questions.

First of all, how in the world did these two reporters convince 33 former UK basketball players from Hall's entire 13-year tenure as head coach to sit down with them and answer questions on tape about cheating and corruption in the UK basketball program?

I don't know. Could it be that players had been receiving money from boosters nonstop since before Beard, Groza, Barnstable, Line, Hirsch, and Spivey all took those handouts, plus the money from bookies and gamblers? Why hide something everyone has known about for 40 years? Of the 33 players interviewed, 26 admitted to receiving frequent payments from various boosters, while 31 of them admitted to having knowledge that this sort of thing went on all the time. These players received what they called "hundred-dollar handshakes" from boosters in the locker room after games. Many players had one specific booster that they were paired with shortly after their arrival on campus, kind of like the senior-buddy program at West Beverly that paired Harold with Steve Sanders and led to Steve using Harold to help him change his grades to get into USC. These special boosters were often referred to as the player's "sugar daddy," a phrase that is incredibly creepy in that it conjures images of, well, I'll let you conjure your own images of the quid for that particular pro quo.

Secondly, how did these reporters get some of these boosters to talk to them?

I have no idea. Especially after a dozen boosters were barred from contact in 1976, and booster payouts had led, in part, to NCAA sanctions on two separate occasions. One of the most prominently mentioned boosters, Maynard Hogg,[34] an Eastern Kentucky coal operator, was the sugar daddy for UK player Fred Cowan, who played between 1977 and 1981.[35] Neither Hogg nor Cowan felt any shame at giving or receiving ~~these payments. Hogg claimed that~~ the money represented deferred

[34] I know, right. That is maybe the most perfect name for a corrupt UK booster ever imagined. I don't think he had much choice in the matter. He was locked into this path the moment his lovin' mother give him that unfortunate handle.

[35] Does that mean he was getting paid to play on an NCAA Championship team? You bet it does.

payments to Cowan for a summer job, which is possibly the lamest excuse ever given for anything, except that it's eerily similar to Rupp's excuse for the money his players received three years after their participation in the London Olympics.

Cowan said Hogg would give him "a couple hundred dollars ... anytime he wanted it."

Among the other players on the 1978 team who admitted to receiving money were Scott Courts, Kyle Macy, and Jay Schidler. One player on that championship team who claimed to have no knowledge of anyone receiving any payout for anything was guard Dwane Casey.[36] Casey also defended the coaching staff saying, in effect, that there's no way a coaching staff can know everything that their boosters and players are doing.

Third, why in all of God's green goodness would Joe B. Hall need 322 free tickets to every home game?

I have no idea, but that's how many he got. The players got tickets too, and you know what they did with them? If you said sold them for a profit against NCAA regulations, award yourself 10 points.

One player, Jay Schidler, sold his tickets to Joe B. Hall's attorney, Cecil Dunn, because it's clear Hall really needed 323 tickets. Schidler, realizing the value of these tickets, upped the price on Dunn each year. Dunn, aside from being Joe B's friend and attorney worked for the Fayette County attorney's office, and one of the many things they did at the Fayette County attorney's office was enforce Kentucky's ticket scalping laws.[37]

---

[36] Though there are reasons to doubt his credibility, as we'll see soon enough.

Fourth, Where's the best place to eat in Lexington if you were a basketball player for Joe B. Hall?

This one I've got. Cliff Hagan's Ribeye, where players and their dates frequently got free meals, which is against NCAA regulations. Well, how the hell is Cliff Hagan supposed to know that? He's just the owner of a local eatery and UK fan. Oh, and he was on the 1951 National Championship point shaving team, but he only played three season because NCAA violations stripped him of his senior season. Well, that doesn't mean he was aware of NCAA rules. You might argue that playing for Rupp would make it considerably less likely that he'd know any rules (or black people). But wait, Hagan was the UK athletic director in 1985. Yeah, then he should have known better.

Fifth, speaking of Hagan, who was in charge of making sure all this corruption, you know hundred-dollar handshakes, ticket scalping, free meals, didn't happen?

I have no idea. And neither did anyone at UK. The president said it was Hagan, who said it was Joe B. There was no supervision from the athletic department and no compliance office, which wasn't rare at the time. It was all on the back of the coach to ensure the rules weren't violated.

Sixth, how did Joe B. go about ensuring that no rules were violated? He handed out a memo to his players every year explaining what the rules were. Done and done.

Seventh, what about UK guard Melvin Turpin?

Yeah, what about Melvin Turpin? That's exactly what Melvin said.
[37] I can't define irony, but I know it when I see it.

Turpin said he never got any handouts while he was at UK, despite being one of their best players. And you know what? He was pretty pissed about it. "I was one of their top players, and they didn't even hardly help me at all," he told the *Herald-Leader*. He was still so mad a year after he left UK that he said, "I ain't speaking with Kentucky at all, because of how they did me and stuff."

And the last question I had was what became of all of this and why don't I remember any of it? The NCAA launched an investigation less than a week after the articles were published to address why players had been paid to play for more than 13 years. As the investigation progressed, the *Herald-Leader* reported its findings, one of which being that Dave Batton, a UK recruit in 1973 who ended up playing at Notre Dame, was offered $20,000 to attend UK by booster Seth Hancock, owner of Claiborne Farms.

The NCAA investigation of these player-admitted violations went from October 1985 to March 1988 then ceased, possibly because the NCAA had bigger fish to fry.

In autumn 1985 Hoosier star Steve Alford, a junior at the time, posed for a charity calendar for a campus sorority, which violated NCAA rules. Similarly, former Ohio State quarterback, Mike Tomczak modeled clothing for a department store and was paid for it in 1983. He and Ohio State got a reprimand for it.

Clearly Alford's mistake was graver than Tomczak's as Alford was given a one-game suspension and two days prior to the IU versus UK game, the NCAA announced that Alford's suspension was to be served against UK. The ridiculousness of this was not lost on Knight who said, "I thought it was a tremendous irony, with all the garbage that's gone on in Kentucky over the years that this happens prior to that particular basketball game."

The hypocrisy colored Knight's opinion of the yearly Kentucky game. Knight told longtime Wildcat broadcaster, Cawood Ledford, that "This game, because of all that's transpired down here over the years with recruiting, and all the crap that's happened here, it isn't nearly so special to me as you might think."

As a soon to be 10 year-old, I was mad that Alford was suspended for the game. I was completely unaware of the *Herald-Leader* article, but I knew my coach thought UK was full of cheaters, so I did, too. And it burned that we lost to UK because of this ruling.

During the two-and-a-half-years the NCAA investigated these violations, which were printed in the newspaper and never recanted by any of the players, they adopted minimum grade standards for incoming freshmen. The rule, known as Proposition 48, or Prop 48, mandated that incoming freshmen must have a 2.0 grade point average in 11 core classes in high school and score a 700 on the SAT or a 15 on the ACT. In other words, incoming freshmen had to score in the 18th percentile and clear the Mendoza line.

No new rules were made to govern boosters or compliance.

The NCAA requested the tapes the *Herald-Leader* made of the interviews with the 33 former players, and the *Herald-Leader* bravely said no.

This refusal, combined with the Hallian approach UK took to helping the NCAA in the investigation (they sent letters informing people that the NCAA would like to talk to them and the university needed to know whether they would or wouldn't agree to speak with the NCAA, thus ensuring that they would not agree).

Kentucky completed their half-assed self-investigation in March 1986 and impatiently awaited the conclusion of the NCAA investigation.

After two more years of investigating, the NCAA was only able to come up with one source who would confirm statements made in the *Herald-Leader*, effectively scuttling the investigation, but that didn't stop them from not telling anyone what they found out.

On March 4, 1988 the NCAA concluded their investigation by doing absolutely nothing. With very public reports of over 13 years of athletes being paid to play for UK the most the NCAA could find them guilty of was not being very helpful in the investigation. Kentucky received a reprimand. That's it.

So, why would the *Herald-Leader* go to all the trouble to convince these players and boosters to admit on the record that they had cheated for over a decade and then refuse to aid the investigation their own article started?

I have no idea. But thanks to their refusal, nothing happened to UK and that lack of a major violation would be the greatest gift ever given to Kentucky basketball because it severely diminished the penalties their next round of cheating would bring about.

Remember Dwane Casey, the only player interviewed who not only had never seen anyone take any money, but didn't blame the coaches for not knowing about it either? After all it's pretty hard to know everything that's going on in your program. What the hell did you want Joe B to do? He sent out a memo.

Eddie Sutton, when he replaced Hall in the midst of this investigation, brought Casey on as an assistant coach and made him one of his lead recruiters. So, he went from player to coach, just like Joe B. Kentucky had a long history of embracing their past and bringing it forward into the present. Joe B was a player on a national championship cheating team. So was athletic director Cliff Hagan. Dwane Casey fit that mold perfectly.

The Hundred Dollar Handshake Investigation ended with a whimper on March 4, 1988, pushing away what Eddie Sutton referred to as a "dark cloud" hanging over the program.

On April 14, 1988 a package from Dwane Casey to Claud Mills, the father of prized recruit Chris Mills, a California senior who had recently inked his letter of intent to join the Wildcats in the fall of 1988 popped open at an Emery Worldwide Air Freight office in California, revealing a videotape of UK's midnight madness and $1,000.

If the people of Kentucky thought the previous three years were bad, they were going to be considerably less pleased with the doings about to transpire.

Casey admitted to putting the videotape in the envelope and placing it on a secretary's desk. He claimed it was open when he put it on her desk and that he had not put any money in it. The secretary, for her part, couldn't say whether the envelope had been sealed when it was placed on her desk, but that it was sealed when Emery picked it up.

The package arrived sealed in California, but opened while being handled. An Emery employee saw the money and alerted his supervisor who counted the fifty $20 bills. This was witnessed by five other employees and the money was counted by at least one other employee before being placed back in the envelope, which was then resealed and delivered. Claud Mills claimed to have received the package, but denied that there was any money in it.

The next day UK hired outside council to help guide their investigation, having learned their lesson from the severe hand-slapping they receive a month earlier from the NCAA.

That same day, the immediate and predictable response from UK fans, and strangely the parents of athletes that UK was recruiting, was that this must be some kind of setup.

It took Casey fewer than four days to hire his own attorney, Joe Bill Campbell, who immediately threatened to sue UK if they scapegoated his client and Emery for finding and reporting the contents of the envelope, on which his client had written his own name on the return address line. He also threatened to sue the employees of Emery for looking inside the package, for opening it on purpose, and maybe for planting the money there themselves in an effort to get Mills to back out of his commitment to UK and sign with UCLA. The primary basis for his case, that they opened the package on purpose, was the result of an experiment he did on a package where he "put a videotape in an envelope and threw it on the floor ten times." After this abuse "it was as tightly sealed ... as when I first sealed it." MYTH BUSTED!

He then threatened to sue the makers of the videotape for it breaking into pieces spontaneously, Andrew Jackson for appearing on the $20 bill, The U.S. Mint for making $20 bills so readily available, the secretary at UK for mailing the package Casey instructed her to mail, and Casey himself, just to make sure all his bases were covered.

Eddie Sutton spent as much time as he could not talking about any of this mess, a strategy that largely worked, as he escaped blame and responsibility for failing to supervise his staff, but ultimately not the consequences of being the buck stopper.

On April 20, 1988, Billy Reed, a columnist for the *Herald-Leader* wrote an article laying the blame for this situation squarely where it belonged; on UK fans and the culture of the program that has allowed decades of cheating. This article was published well before all the facts were known. In the article, he said that "the sad notion that Wildcat basketball is more important than anything" was at heart of the problem.

Reed cited Judge Saul Streit's statement from the trial following the point shaving scandal in 1952 in which Streit charged that "UK subsidized its basketball program in violation of amateur rules, gave athletic scholarships to unqualified students, condoned a climate in which players were 'demoralized' and tolerated supporters who often gave $50 as a reward for winning efforts." Saul Streit, meet Joe B. Hall, Dwane Casey, Cliff Hagan, and Eddie Sutton. I'd also like to introduce you to Chris Mills, Lawrence Funderburke, Shawn Kemp, Sean Woods, and Eric Manuel.

Some of those names should look pretty familiar to Hoosier fans. Shawn Kemp and Sean Woods were both Indiana kids who signed to play at UK with Chris Mills. Both Kemp and Woods were Prop 48 kids, ruled ineligible to play their freshman years because of subpar academic performance in high school. Woods went on to weather the storm at UK, but Kemp never played a minute for Kentucky or any other college program before going on to the NBA and fathering roughly 1,000 children.

Lawrence Funderburke's UK recruitment came under scrutiny during the investigation that followed the $1,000 package. The NCAA eventually leveled 18 charges against UK. Of those 18, the role UK booster Bill Chupil played in transporting Funderburke to Lexington for recruiting trips was central to three of them. Funderburke eventually came to Indiana where he played until a practice on December 14 of his freshman year, when Knight kicked him out. Funderburke left before the rest of the team came into the locker room after practice was over. He wasn't seen on campus again and university officials didn't seem to know where he had gone. By Christmas 1989, news broke that Funderburke wanted to be released from his scholarship and that he wouldn't be returning to Indiana. When it seemed that Funderburke wanted to transfer to Kentucky, Knight refused to allow his release and Kentucky athletic Director C.M. Newton said Funderburke would never be a scholarship or walk-on at UK for many reasons, "mentioned and unmentioned." Funderburke eventually ended up at Ohio State where he had a very good college career.

Eric Manuel was a Kentucky freshman who played for Eddie Sutton in 1987-1988. In July 1988 a few months into the Casey investigation, a report surfaced that the NCAA had questions about Manuel's ACT score. Manuel had taken the test twice and had yet to get the minimum 15 to become eligible. On his third try, with fellow UK recruit and coach's son Sean Sutton taking the test in the same room, many rows away, Manuel managed to pull a 23, which was not only well above the national average, but well above the average increase seen from students taking the test for their third time.

Under the pressure of the NCAA investigation and the possibility that he would be ruled ineligible, Manuel volunteered to sit out of practices and games in the upcoming 1988-1989 season until he was cleared of all accusations; a late 80's version of the Bill Spivey approach.

Manuel's ACT scores were the subject of two of the violations, one

90

for academic fraud and one for providing false information to the NCAA investigators. When the dust settled and UK had responded to the allegations, the NCAA ruled that Manuel had cheated and that he and Sean Sutton lied about who took them to take the test that day. The NCAA had also ruled that Casey had mailed Mills $1,000, noting that Casey was found to have "acted contrary to the principles of ethical conduct, demonstrated a knowing and willful effort to …operate the university's intercollegiate basketball program contrary to the requirements and provisions…." He also provided "false and misleading information" to just about everybody.

Casey was hit with a show-cause order, which meant that if any NCAA member school wanted to hire him for the next five years they had to appeal to the NCAA for permission and show cause why he should be allowed to coach there.

UK was punished with three years of probation, a two-year postseason ban and a one-year television ban. Eddie Sutton and Cliff Hagan quit before they were fired. And university president David Roselle, who started his tenure right before this happened and spent his entire time at UK shepherding the school through the investigation, decided he'd had enough and resigned to take the president's job at Delaware shortly after the investigation was over.

Reed was almost 100 percent right in the blame he laid a week into the investigation. The fans were the ones who allowed coach after coach to cheat and be investigated by the NCAA and put on probation, while still buying tickets and showing up in droves for home games. Where he got it wrong was that the over-importance placed on basketball was not to blame for the atmosphere of cheating and corruption. The fact that winning was more important than anything at Kentucky was to blame.

Rupp was allowed to be a cheater and a racist because he won. Hall was allowed to cheat and allow fans to pay his players and give them free meals because he played for Rupp and he won. Sutton was allowed to run a dirty program because he had Kenny Walker and Rex Chapman. He wasn't a child of the program, but he won so whatever he did was just fine with the Wildcat faithful.

It's a program that for 40 years celebrated wins on the court, paid their players, offered illegal enticements to recruits, and thumbed their noses at the NCAA and all other member schools. And at any point in this illustrious history, if you brought up any of these facts to a typical UK fan you would have been accused of being jealous and been given a number of excuses why no one there did anything wrong. Kentucky and the Wildcat fan[38]38 represent everything I'm against in sports. So yes, I hate Kentucky.

And I'm not the only one.

Mike Davis hated Kentucky. You know how I know? He once said something very telling, something which, while not obvious to all, tipped me off. He said, "I hate Kentucky."

He hated them for ruining his Christmas three years in a row by beating us senseless in the last game before Christmas from 2000 to 2002. It seemed that whatever methods of motivation Mike Davis used, he just couldn't beat UK.

His first year, after losing, he told the press that maybe he was the wrong person to coach this team. Nothing motivates a team like the coach's self-pity, but it didn't get to this group. So the next year, he tried

[38] I'm friends with a few UK fans who are nice, rational people but they aren't above giving these responses either.

running on to the court during the game and hitting himself in the head. When this didn't work, he told the press that he hated UK. In December, 2003 he tried losing to UK by 40 points in an attempt to, I presume, tire them out for the game the following year.

He didn't seem convinced that lying down like dogs would get it done so he did the only thing he could think to do. He moved the game up a week and half. That way, when we lost there'd still be a chance to win a game prior to Christmas. It worked like a charm. In 2004 when we lost to them by 25 on December 11 we had two more chances to grab a win and save Christmas.

We then lost to Missouri and Charlotte. That year Christmas wasn't ruined by UK. It was ruined by clocks that weren't synced properly and a poor review angle that made it possible for a player to catch a pass at half court, pivot, dribble, and shoot in .07 seconds. It was a long way to go to make sure UK didn't ruin Christmas, but it worked.

It took some bad losses, but eventually Davis's hatred and scheduling tactics resulted in a win. On December 10, 2005, we beat UK 79-53.

His hate had made him powerful.

You can imagine the hate-filled joy at my creamy center when we drew the Billy Packer-Verne Lundquist pairing for this year's UK game. I was able to dip a cup into my well of hate and drink deep of the brew that dwelled therein. I drank deep and I drank long, until my thirst was sated. I let the hate flow through me.

But I was nervous. I'd learned a lot about hate, mainly through *Star Wars;* I learned that "fear leads to anger. Anger leads to hate. Hate leads to suffering;" I learned that "anger, fear, aggression, the Dark Side of the Force are they;" I learned that if you strike someone down with all your hatred your journey toward the Dark Side is complete. What happens, then, when what you hate is the Dark Side?

I couldn't imagine that hatred of UK would at some point suck me through the looking glass and make me a UK fan, nor would my hatred of Billy Packer turn me into Billy Packer, but Luke hated the Emperor and what he represented and Palpatine seemed quite sure that this show of hatred would lead Luke over to embrace what he hated.

Of course the Emperor ended up thrown into the power core by Darth Vader,[39] so there was a 20 percent chance that he was wrong.[40]

Aside from the deep, naughty tingle of anticipation I felt at getting to enjoy a hate convergence I was also glad we could put behind us the horrible guard shortage of 2007. It had been worrying Sampson after the Tennessee State game, but he assured us that EJ wasn't hurt that bad and Crawford would be returning from his three game suspension in time to play his older brother Joe.

But Guard Shortage 2007 was such a huge success it was held over for another game. EJ was hurt worse than Sampson either knew or let on after the Tennessee State game and he would be missing the UK game. And while it was true that Crawford would return from his three game rip, it was equally true that Bassett would be taking his turn on the DNP-Suspended line of the box score. Bassett was also suspended for an unspecified violation of team rules.

---

[39] Spoiler Alert!!!!

[40] Packer Method. Damn, does using his method mean I am become Packer, the destroyer of worlds?

I'm not one to make wild unfounded accusations, but I'm not opposed to very reasonable unfounded accusations. Is it possible that in the five days between the end of Crawford's suspension and the UK game Bassett committed a separate but identically serious offense as Crawford? Sure, it's possible. Is it also possible that Bassett and Crawford were up to something stupid together and Sampson decided to give them each a three-game suspension, but rather than go into a tough three game stretch with only two guards (EJ and Jarmarcus), he decided to stagger the suspensions? Yes.

The Sampson Syllogism tells us that good result = good action. And after the Tennessee State game, Sampson said, "When I made the decision to discipline Jordan, we knew these three games were going to be tough. I'm really happy we're 3-0. I mean, we won all three games. That's the most important thing to me."

If winning really was the most important thing to Sampson, as he said, the thought that he'd gear his disciplinary decisions toward that end seems much more likely than a decision to sit half of our guards for a three game stretch. We all know how much he didn't like playing shorthanded in the back court.

In the end, guard injuries and suspensions had no impact on the outcome of the games. We won those three games and we handled Kentucky as expected, so any decision to stagger the suspensions that may or may not have been made did not prevent us from winning, so it was clearly a good decision. As was the decision to put EJ back in the Tennessee State game in the first half with two fouls. These decisions didn't equal losses so they must have been good ones. They only served to further blur the line between doing what is right and what is expedient.

Crawford and Ellis played 39 and 35 minutes, respectively.

Crawford, in his only college match up against his older brother, Joe, came up huge, scoring 20 points on 5-10 shooting (3-5 from three) and 7-10 free throw shooting, while his brother struggled to score 10 points on 4-15 shooting. DJ posted another double-double in another impressive outing. We vanquished UK easily on route to a 70-51 win.

And Packer confounded yet again. Four minutes into the game, after we were called for a questionable charge, Packer announced that hand-checking would be a big story in the game. It wasn't. He then followed that wild unfounded prediction with the assertion that the fact that UK won seven titles with different coaches was an indicator of how strong the program is. I would argue that seven national titles were an indicator of the strength of a program. Having different coaches involved doesn't enter into it. By that reasoning UCLA is not a strong program because 10 of their 11 titles were won by one coach.

I would also argue that UK only had three titles, as they had players involved in point shaving in 1948, 1949, and 1951 as well as players being paid by boosters in 1978, leaving only 1958, 1996, and 1998 as championships won by teams that weren't cheating.

With three minutes to go in the half, Crawford, while being guarded closely by his brother, stepped on the half court line and turned the ball over. He made that mistake, according to Billy, because he's a freshman, which makes perfect sense. It's a well known fact that backcourt violations are not usually taught until junior year.

Basketball is a game of two halves and Packer knew you can't do all of your crazy in the first 20 minutes. He liked to hold a little treat for later. In a game that was not, as far as I could tell, part of the Big Ten/ACC Challenge, he held court on the value of the Big Ten/ACC Challenge. He claimed that inter-conference challenges like the Big Ten/ACC Challenge played a role on Selection Sunday. He contended that the outcome of the challenge was a determining factor in how many teams a league gets in to the tournament in relation to the other league (i.e. the ACC won again, so they would get more teams into the tournament).

You know why that sounds crazy? Because it's nearly 100 percent wrong. When Packer said that the ACC had won every Big Ten/ACC Challenge since its inception in the 1999-2000 season, would you care to guess in how many of those years the ACC had more teams in the tournament than the Big Ten?

One.

That's it. Every other year the Big Ten presence was greater than or equal to the ACC presence. It took me about 10 minutes to fact check that, which is why the Packer Method is used by 68 percent of the population. It's a big time saver It took him zero minutes to make a crazy assertion.

After beating Kentucky I felt so good about being better than them and handing it to them so easily that, emotionally, I put aside all of my reservations about our shortcomings as a team, the potential character issues that may have shown themselves in two suspensions by early December, the questionable leadership shown by a coach who seemed to be making discipline decisions based on the preservation of winning, and the specter of an NCAA investigation. I enjoyed the win. Beating Kentucky and being 8-1 with enough talent to beat any team in the country was enough for me.

There may be something to the Sampson Syllogism after all. I'm not saying that it is factually correct, but there's a truthiness to it.

I wasn't even that annoyed with Billy Packer. Sure, he was wrong. A lot. But I had started to turn the corner from annoyed to mildly amused by his ass-basketry. I had even embraced the Packer Method. I knew in my head that something wasn't right, but my gut was feeling pretty good about our record.

Interlude Five: A Study, In General

One of things I love about CBS' coverage of college basketball is when a player is on the free throw line getting ready to shoot, they put a graphic in the lower third with the player's name and number as well as some other information, like free throw percentage, season averages, or my all-time favorite, college major.

This is such a ridiculous thing to put on the screen. As we all know only 10 to 15 percent of them would even get in to college without sports.[41] And 90 percent of college athletes major in general studies,[42] 10 percent major in sports management,[43] and 8 percent major in something else.

I just don't care that Stemler is a general studies major. I really don't care what EJ's major is. His plan was always to play one year and jump to the NBA, which is to be expected. He was in college to prepare to get a job; one year would be all the preparation he required, and while it was important for him to attend classes and do well in the classroom, my knowledge of his declared major was completely unnecessary.

I remember that Alan Henderson was pre-med. You know where he went to med school? The Atlanta Hawks. From all accounts Alan was a good student who was an Academic All-Big Ten player in 1993, but what mattered to us was that he was an All-American basketball player in 1995.

Kyle Hornsby was a four-time Academic All-Big Ten player. I

---

[41] Original use of Packer Method

[42] Packer Method

[43] ibid

don't know what his major was. I think he was pre-med as well, but I don't know and I don't care. He was the type of player we love at IU. He played hard and had possibly the purest jump shot I've ever seen.

The only player I saw all season for IU that was listed in a game as anything other than a general studies major is that show-off Brett Finkelmeier, who is lording it over everyone by majoring in biology and preparing to be a dentist. What an asshole.

Student majors are not in the media guide. They don't mention it because no one cares. IU fans care that the team is performing well academically, that the team is meeting APR (though none of us could tell you how APR is determined). We don't care what classes they are taking.

I can tell you for a fact the Harris Mujezinovic did not take the History of the Democratic Party taught by Dr. Irving Katz as I was in that class and he dropped it after three classes. Past that, I got nothin'. And I'm fine with that.

There are people I went to college with who are very good friends of mine whose college majors I do not know. You know why? Because it doesn't matter. I was a history/political science major. I'm a grade school principal and I'm writing a book about Indiana basketball. I have a good friend who was a theatre-lighting design major. He builds websites. I have another friend who was a history major, I think. Now he works for the Indiana State Libraries as, I believe, a "transponster." For most people their major doesn't matter two years or in some cases two months after you finish your degree. The important thing is that you work hard, learn from your classes, learn how to learn and work both independently and as part of a group. Armed with that knowledge, why do I care what DJ's major is?

Chapter Six: The Valedictorian of Summer School

I am the product of Catholic education. If my grad work counts, and who's to say it doesn't, we're talking 20 years of Catholic education. That brings with it all of the things you would expect it to bring; love of uniforms, fear of penguins, and a deep personal connection to *Only the Good Die Young.* And one you probably wouldn't, unless you played for the St. Anthony Bears in the late 1980s, which was my overinflated sense of my own basketball skills.

The Bears were a powerhouse. We were a championship team my seventh and eighth grade years. We won the deanery both years and in my eighth grade year we were one ridiculous late game collapse from making the Final Four. We had three guys on the team over six feet tall and a point guard who had flunked fourth grade. Do you know how big of an advantage it is to have a kid who flunked a grade on your team? It's huge. That extra year of physical, if not intellectual, maturity means a great deal when everyone else on your team is going through the awkward effects of growth spurts pretty much all the time. We had strong play at the other guard positions. We were unguardable.

We had some great battles, including a deanery championship game against Holy Family where we took the lead on a baseline runner with four seconds left and sealed the victory when I stole the inbounds pass and dribbled out the clock.[44]

We were great. We were better than Holy Family and Sacred Heart. We were a lot better than Our Lady of Perpetual Help and we made St. Mary's and St. Joseph's look like, well, junior high basketball teams.

In my eighth grade mind a montage set to "Eye of the Tiger" played in which we wore our gold trunks and gloves while we easily

---

[44] I actually intercepted a pass at half court and drove it uncontested to the basket where I took an ill-advised layup that I put right into the bottom of the rim, but don't tell anybody. It sounds cooler if I dribbled out the clock.

dispatched the likes of Joe Czak and Big Yank Ball in places like Radio City Music Hall and Caesar's Palace. We beat the German Champ in London while capturing the hearts of European fans. We appeared on the cover of *The Ring* magazine, *Tempo*, *L'Uomo Vogue*, *People*, *Newsweek*, *Inside Sports,* and *GQ*. We published our own scrapbook. We filmed American Express commercials. We raised at least $343,638 for charity. We bought motorcycles and fur coats, hawked DeLorians, Nikon Cameras, Amoco, Maserati, Tony Lamas jeans, Gatorade, Budweiser, and Crunch Punch candy bars. We appeared on the *Muppet Show* and had our photo taken with Gerald Ford, Bob Hope, Jimmy Carter, and Ronald Reagan. We put our likeness on T-shirts, coffee mugs, high ball glasses, and dinnerware. Our hometown erected a statue of us on the steps of the art museum. But it was a house of deception built on a foundation of lies. We'd been carried. And we didn't even know it.

We only played other Catholic schools. We didn't play the larger, public schools that were all around us where they had kids who were upwards of 6'5. They had multiple kids who could dribble with both hands. They had kids who had funked two grades![45]

If we had played the public schools during those years we would have played the likes of B.J. Flynn, who played for Louisville; Sheron Wilkerson who was named, ever so briefly, Indiana's Mr. Basketball in 1993, then went to play at IU until things went wrong for him and he was kicked off the team; Brad Bixler, who went on to play for Bellarmine; and Brent Conner, Brien Hanley, and Cory Norman who went on to play at Rose Hullman, Xavier, and Western Carolina, respectively. All of those players played on the 1993 Indiana State Championship team. From my seventh and eighth grade teams the number of players who played college basketball was 0.0.

---

[45] I don't know that at all, but some of those kids were BIG.

How could we compete with that? We couldn't, and the proof of that was on display every Friday and Saturday night when Providence High School, the school into which all deanery schools fed, faced off against Jeffersonville and New Albany or any school where the public junior high schools fed, the Providence Pioneers almost always lost.

That there was some kind of connection to be drawn between Providence's losses against the public high schools and our potential success against the public junior high schools had not occurred to us, dude.

One could look at the Hoosiers (8-1) after the UK game and feel ready to announce our retirement on the steps of the Philadelphia Museum of Art. That record reflected success over adversity. We'd won those games through two suspensions, injuries to EJ, Bassett, DJ, and Crawford and we didn't even have AJ Ratliff on the team yet. And our adversity was far from overcome. Prior to the Western Carolina game, freshman center Eli Holman broke his hand and was likely out for the rest of the season. We were heading into a three-game fontanel on our schedule that would lead us into Big Ten play and we had yet to play a game with our full roster. And with Eli likely done for the year, it didn't look like we were ever going to.

In our next three games we dispatched of Western Carolina, Coppin State, and Chicago State by an average of 38 points per game, but not without suffering another injury. During the Chicago State game Bassett suffered a bone chip that was likely going to require surgery. It wouldn't prevent him from playing, but he wouldn't be 100 percent for the rest of the season.

Maybe we were even better than our 11-1 nonconference record and spotty play indicated. Maybe finding ways to win in spite of these

104

injuries and suspensions was reason to hope that once AJ came back from his present self-inflicted street-clothes status we might be able to bring our game to another level and compete for a national title.

Or maybe something else was going on that wasn't quite so shiny.

Coach Sampson said on November 12 prior to the Chattanooga game, "Sometimes your record is a reflection of who you play." He wasn't trying to criticize our opponents. in fact, as he had said on numerous occasions, "We have a great deal of respect for [insert opponent's name here]." He also wasn't trying to say we weren't as good as our record may indicate, but it's hard not to read it that way when you look at our schedule up to that point.

Our nonconference schedule consisted of UT-Chattanooga (8-5), Longwood (4-13), UNC-Wilmington (8-6), Illinois State (10-3), Xavier (10-3), Georgia Tech (6-6), Southern Illinois (6-7), Tennessee State (4-8), Kentucky (6-6), Western Carolina (4-9), Coppin State (3-11), and Chicago State (5-12).[46] That is a combined total of (74-89). We only played two games against a Top 25 team; Illinois State, a ranking that was largely based on how good their team had been the previous year, and Xavier, which wasn't ranked in the Top 25 when we played them. And we lost to Xavier. It's hard not to look at that list and think we were the Farmer Ted of college basketball, King of the Dipshits.

After our three-game-home-stand against Western Carolina, Coppin State, and Chicago State the fact that we had played what would end up being the 62nd hardest schedule in college basketball according to the Sagarin ratings for 2007-2008 had not escaped the more observant members of the press corps, one of whom had the temerity to ask

---

[46] All records as of January 3, 2008.

Sampson about it.

Reporter: "Kelvin, you haven't played a team with a winning record in a while. Do you really feel that this schedule is readying your team for what's coming ahead here?"

Sampson: "Yes. [Long Pause] Do you?"

Reporter: "Seriously?" *I can't believe he's going grade school on me here. If he says he's rubber and I'm glue, I'm leaving.* "I'm wondering..."

Sampson is nothing if not a Renaissance man of avoidance. Here you will see the second example of him employing the Leon Black method of interview control. The reporters start out by asking him questions and he answers a few, at which point he flips it and starts asking them questions.

He tried this once before with a student who asked him about sealing the state borders and it worked perfectly; the kid folded and told him he was doing a great job.

Sampson: "What do you wonder?"

Reporter: *Exactly what I just asked you, you bloated sack of crap.* "Well, it's a whole different league. I just don't think these teams are of the caliber you're going to face here in the next couple of weeks."

Sampson: "Well, um, is that unusual, from the other teams in the country?"

Here you see a slight shift in tactics. He's still employing the Leon Black method, but he's including in his reversal a "But Mom! Everybody else is doing it!" position.

106

Reporter: "Sometimes you get a holiday tournament that's a little bit more competitive."

Sampson: "Yeah, well, when we set the schedule up we said we're playing Kentucky at home, Georgia Tech at Southern Illinois, who else did we play?"

This is a textbook use of a list as a diversion. The idea behind this is to confuse the questioner with a series of names that sounds impressive and may fool him into thinking his question was without merit.

Voice: "Xavier."

Sampson: "Xavier, Illinois State. Maybe you should give us a little credit."

The defense here is simple. Our schedule is fine. Everyone else schedules these cupcakes. We scheduled a whole list of good teams. Give us some credit for how good our schedule is. Besides, like I said, everyone schedules like this.

It is unclear the minimum qualifications Sampson sets for the giving and receiving of credit, but "We didn't know they were all going to be bad, except for Xavier," is just a hair above the Mendoza line.

The "But Mom! Everybody else is doing it!" rationale is made even weaker than normal since it is clear that Sampson seems to know that everyone else is, in fact, not doing it. Moments after defending our schedule, he said, "That's a great win Wisconsin had today against Texas."

Wisconsin, unranked, instead of playing Coppin State on a 12-hour turnaround and all night road trip, traveled to Austin to play ninth ranked

Texas. They came out with a win and valuable experience winning road games against tough opponents on late game three-pointers.

It would be a real shame if this experience came back to bite us in the ass, while our experience of beating teams by 38 sat there unused as the season wound down. There were a number of other schools playing stiff competition at this time of year, including Georgetown, Michigan State, and Memphis, though to be fair Memphis' overall schedule was almost as bad as ours (58th).

It is still unclear why this bothers me so much. We have always scheduled our late December games against less than stellar competition and it never bothered me before. And Sampson was right; pretty much everyone else was doing it this way. The major difference between everyone else and us—this year and every other year— is that we were supposed to be better than that. We should have been comparing ourselves to what the best teams were doing, not what most teams were doing.

We had the talent to do anything, but without being tested at all, our record seemed to be a traveshamockery. These last three games held true to form with stretches of bad play and lopsided wins. In the second game we played Coppin State at noon on a Saturday after they played a late game on Friday in Milwaukee. Coppin State got on the bus, drove the seven hours or so down to Bloomington, presumably slept on the bus, and played us within two points, 28-26, at halftime. It was the bizzarro half. Coppin State looked like the 9-1 team that slept at home in their beds and we looked like the 3-9 squad who slept on the bus and should have been betting Crash that he couldn't get us a rain out. But we won, so it was good.

We were halfway through the season and I wasn't sure how good

108

we were. That's a strange place to be. On one hand, we had an average margin of victory of 24.5 points and an 11-1 record. On the other hand, we had played a very soft schedule and had yet to play to our ability for a full game. We'd been subject to injuries and suspensions, and our coach seemed more interested in explaining away the negatives than addressing what could turn into a very real problem.

Sampson frequently said things like, "I thought the second half was really good,"[47] along with gems like "I couldn't have asked for a better 17 minutes to start the game,"[48] "I thought we got off to a great start,"[49] and "The story of that game is the second half."[50]

He also repeatedly showed his adherence to the Sampson Syllogism of win = good, lose = bad. "I don't mind threes as long as they go in. You shoot 30 times, you're not making any, probably not a good idea, but if you shoot 30 and are making 18, I'd say they're pretty good shots,"[51] and "These kind of games tell you things, but the most important thing about this game is that we won it,"[52] and other comments like "When the ball goes in, your offense is pretty good,"[53] and "I'm not really into analyzing this game. We won it. A month from now, it's going to be a W,"[54] and

[47] Coppin State

[48] Tennessee State

[49] Xavier

[50] Chattanooga

[51] Pembroke

[52] Illinois State

[53] Xavier, again

[54] Tennessee State, again

"When I made the decision to discipline Jordan, we knew these three games were going to be tough. We're 3-0. I mean, we won all three games. That's the most important thing to me."[55] And another insightful classic: "Ball goes in, your offense is pretty good. It doesn't, it looks like there's something wrong."[56]

Looking at the season through the prism of the Sampson Syllogism, he must have been ecstatic. We were getting ready to enter Big Ten play at 11-1 and ranked 12th in the nation.

For me, the bloom had come off the rose a little. The joy I was feeling after beating Kentucky had turned to disquiet. I wasn't sure who this team was that I was rooting for. Thus far, we had a lot of blowout wins against St. Mary's and St. Joseph's. We handled Our Lady of Perpetual Help and Sacred Heart pretty well, and we lost our one matchup with Holy Family. We might have been pretty good, but I was pretty nervous about what would happen when we had to play the kids from the public schools.

---

[55] Once more, Tennessee State

[56] Coppin State, again

Interlude Six: "Nine Misfortunes? I'd Like to See That"

Superstition plays a major role in sports. Some players have a specific set of rituals bordering on the Melvin Udall when a batter steps into the box. *cough* Nomar *cough.* It is widely held that you don't talk to a pitcher while he's in the middle of a no-hitter, presumably because isolation and an intense feeling of being all by yourself are the best ways to ensure success. Athletes often imbue their jersey numbers with special mythical qualities.

Some superstitions don't have anything to do with the athlete directly. There's the Madden Curse; every player to appear on the cover of the video game Madden NFL since the appearance of Steve McNair in 1999 has been either injured that season or performed well below expectations.

Stephen King quits shaving at the end of baseball season, grows a full beard in mourning of the season, and then shaves it at the start of the next season. What he thought this accomplished, as he is a Red Sox fan and stuck with that same ritual for 30 years before the Red Sox won anything, is a bit of a mystery to me, but that's kind of the point. Superstitions are illogical and highly personal.

I watched the last 10 minutes of the 1987 Championship game with my hat turned inside out and backwards to inspire a rally by the Hoosiers.[57]

Announcers (Don Fischer comes to mind here) seem to believe that if they mention a free throw shooting streak by a player that streak will end almost immediately thanks to their jinx.

---

[57] And it worked, so shut up!

Religion plays a big role in superstition. Jobu was asked to come and take the fear of the curveball away from Pedro Cerrano's bat, because Jesus Christ is no help with the curveball. Strap said a prayer every time before entering the game. This superstition was so much a part of the team that no one expected him to enter the game before he completed the prayer. Even Coach Dale had to respect it in order to get Strap on the court where God wanted him. He even asked Strap to make it a good one for Ollie.

Rocky stopped by the church on the way to fight Apollo to get a blessing and said a prayer in the corner before each fight.

Countless athletes answer any question asked of them by thanking God. God was very interested in whether Mike Davis won a game. For all God's interest in the winning coach, I would love, just once, for someone to blame God after they lose a game.[58]

Sometimes superstitions are tactile. Players at Notre Dame touch the *Play Like a Champion Today* placard before entering the field of play. Coach Hep had our players touch the Rock. Steve Alford always touched Socks, Hips and Dribbled Thrice before shooting free throws.

All superstitions have two things in common: The first, as Crash Davis said, is that they're all true. "A player has to respect the streak. If you believe you're playing well because you're getting laid or because you're not getting laid or because you wear women's underwear, then you are!" The other thing they all have in common is they are all there to avoid tempting fate.

---

[58] I got my wish when Bills receiver Stevie Johnson blamed God for a dropped pass via tweet 2010. "I PRAISE YOU 24/7!!!!!! AND THIS IS HOW YOU DO ME!!!!! YOU EXPECT ME TO LEARN FROM THIS??? HOW???!!! ILL NEVER FORGET THIS!! EVER! I'm likely to draft him two rounds earlier than he deserves for my Fantasy team, just out of respect.

Mr. Burns didn't know about tempting fate. He told Smithers there was no way his team of major league ringers could lose in their big softball game, "unless, of course, my nine all-stars fall victim to nine separate misfortunes and are unable to play tomorrow. But that will never happen. Three misfortunes, that's possible. Seven misfortunes, there's an outside chance. But nine misfortunes? I'd like to see that!"

He tempted fate, but his team only suffered eight misfortunes and they ended up winning the game.

I learned the lesson about tempting fate the hard way. I got a great Christmas present on December 23, 1989, when UK lost in overtime to SW Louisiana in the UKIT. UK promptly cancelled the UKIT and vowed to never speak of the shortcut again, because it couldn't possibly be that the school was on probation and playing with a severely depleted roster thanks to Dwane Casey and Eddie Sutton. No, it was the tournament's fault. Let's cancel that.

I laughed heartily at all the UK fans I knew because who hosts their own holiday tournament filled with scrubs and loses? Not knowing about tempting fate I laughed and pointed and laughed some more, secure in the knowledge that IU would never lose a game in either the Indiana Classic or the Hoosier Classic.

Six years later, I still had not learned about tempting fate. UK won the National Championship. It was their first championship since 1978. I took solace where I could find it, by telling UK fans to talk to me when IU went 18 years without a title.

On December 20, 2001, we lost to Butler in the Hoosier Classic and I began to feast on my words.

Then 2005 came and went without another championship for IU and I was forced to realize that I shouldn't tempt fate with assertions based on my predictions of the future. It just doesn't end well.

So, no more Hoosier Classic. No more Indiana Classic. We're still playing the same level of competition around Christmas, at home. We're just not calling it a tournament. Lesson learned. No more shooting my mouth off about what will or won't happen with IU basketball. When you tempt fate, sometimes fate punches you in the crotch.

Chapter Seven: If You're Looking For Trouble, You Came to the Right Place

On December 3, 1968, 42 percent of the viewing population tuned in to see something extraordinary. Elvis Presley's face filled the screen as he sneered, "If you're lookin' for trouble, you came to the right place. If you're lookin' for trouble, just look right in my face." Dressed in a black leather suit and red neckerchief (I know. It was 1968. The neckerchief still had some cachet at that point. See Fred from the Scoobie gang), the King of Rock 'N' Roll took the stage for his first performance in seven years. He performed one large set piece and then sat on a small stage surrounded by some of his original band and tore through a set that consisted of some of his best material.

At times during his performance the energy of the music was so strong in him that he tried to stand up, but with the guitar not strapped to his neck and the mic locked in place for a seated performance, he ended up nearly dropping his guitar and having to bend over to sing. He made jokes about his famous curled lips and told a story of how his movements on stage used to be restricted because of the worries over his indecent hips. Then they cut to Elvis on stage by himself, guitar in hand, shaking his hips and dancing, surrounded on the edges of the stage by beautiful women.

He played the elder statesman of rock 'n' roll and talked about the many changes in music over the previous 12 years. He gave his blessing to the new sounds, performers, recording techniques, and sound engineers. He said he liked The Beatles and some of the other groups that were out there and reminded us how rock 'n' roll is basically just an offspring of gospel and rhythm and blues. There was an energy and excitement to his performance that had been lacking since his return from the Army.

When Elvis was drafted into the Army on March 24, 1958, he had already earned his place as the King. He had scored 11 number one hits with another four coming while he was still serving. He was honorably discharged in May 1960. Upon his return, Elvis immediately went into the studio to record six new songs to get a single on the market, including "Stuck on You," a traditional Elvis-style rocker and "Fame and Fortune," a doo-wop number.

This was a watershed moment for the King. He could have chosen to make his return on *American Bandstand* with Dick Clark, with whom he had done a phone interview for his 25th birthday while he was still in the Army, a show geared toward the teenage audience. He could have gone on the *Ed Sullivan Show* as he did in 1956 when he was shot from the waist up to avoid inciting the libidos of teenage girls and as the Beatles would do four years later to introduce themselves to America.

The world waited for the return of the King. And return he did.

On May 12, 1960, Elvis made his televised return from the Army on ABC's *The Frank Sinatra Timex Special* in what was a blatant attempt to bill himself as a pop star and appeal to an older audience. Elvis was introduced by Frank, Sammy, Joey Bishop, Peter Lawford, and Nancy Sinatra who sang him out with a cheesy opening number. He entered wearing his dress blues (or so I assume. It was in black and white…) and all hope that the pre-war Elvis was returning to his sneering, hip-shaking form were all but dashed. He looked tame and ready to try his hand as a pop singer of standards and show tunes.

All hope for the return of cool Elvis was officially gone when he came out in a tuxedo and sang "Fame and Fortune" and "Stuck on You," and then joined Frank for a duet medley of "Love Me Tender" and "Witchcraft." In a stark counterpoint to the shaking hips that drew so much attention in 1956, he and Frank shrugged their shoulder while singing. A move that is both considerably less cool and almost impossible to edit out by locking the camera in above the offending action.

The Elvis of the 1950's was gone. What came back from the Army was a carefully packaged star of horrible movies and songs whose quality matched that of his films.

He only had two number 1 hits after his return, and none after the early part of 1962.

By 1968, Elvis, thanks to the general crappiness of his movies and the extreme crappiness of the music that came from them, had ceased to matter as a musician. In 1956 he was the coolest person on the planet. By 1968 he was largely a joke. Then he came on stage in that black leather suit and put on the type of performance that showed the world once again why he was so *great*. The differences between the two specials were obvious. Instead of an Army uniform and a tuxedo, Elvis wore black leather. Instead of trying to sell his latest single, he performed the songs that made him great.

However, all vestiges of his cheesy post-Army period were not swept away. He performed larger set pieces that felt more like musical theatre than rock 'n' roll. But Elvis was cool again, if just for one night. Elvis was *great*.

Elvis is the perfect example of *greatness*. He proves three things about the nature of greatness in our society: First, anything that stays on the stage for a long time will have moments of greatness interspersed with stretches of mediocrity. Secondly, no one gets to stay on the stage to suffer stretches of mediocrity unless they achieve greatness early. And thirdly, the majority of your career does not have to be great. In fact, much of it can be subpar.

This kind of greatness can be found throughout popular culture. *Saturday Night Live* is a perfect example of this phenomenon in television. *SNL* has been on the air for over 30 years. Of those 30, less than half were *great*.

The first five seasons of *SNL* were *great*. They pushed the envelope for comedy, television, and pop culture. It launched the careers of Bill Murray, Chevy Chase, Dan Akroyd, and John Belushi and helped propel Steve Martin from popular stand-up comedian to a comedy superstar, selling out venues so large he had to wear a white suit on stage just so the audience could see him.

When the original cast left the show after the sixth season, the show was in danger of being cancelled. From 1981 to 1986 the show failed to find anything approaching the same rhythm and greatness the original cast enjoyed. If not for the star power of Eddie Murphy and Joe

118

Piscopo, the show may have ended there.

Established names were brought in to try and save the once relevant show. Billy Crystal, Martin Short, Harry Shearer, Robert Downey, Jr., Christopher Guest, and Anthony Michael Hall all did stints on the show, providing it with some moments of greatness, but the show was not great and had not been for years.

But, in the fall of 1986, the foundation of the next great run was put in place with Dennis Miller, Dana Carvey, John Lovitz, Phil Hartman, and Kevin Nealon. Mike Myers came aboard in 1988, and Chris Farley, Chris Rock, Adam Sandler, David Spade, and Rob Schneider joined the cast in 1991.

This cast started to break apart in 1993, and while there have been moments of brilliance in the years since, Will Ferrell, in general, and Tine Fey's impersonation of Sarah Palin comprising the *SNL* version of *Elvis: The '68 Comeback Special*, it has failed to reach greatness again. These eras of mediocrity do not detract from *SNL's* inherent *greatness*, just as *Blue Hawaii* doesn't detract from Elvis Presley's.

Paul McCartney and the Rolling Stones have shown similar *greatness* arcs over the course of their respective careers; early unparalleled greatness followed by stretches of crappiness with islands of Elvis in black leather puncturing the sea of floating crap.

How much greatness, then, is required to establish oneself as *great*? The answer seems to be different in sports than in entertainment. It takes a lot less, and there is a greater forgiveness of mediocrity in entertainment than there is in sports.

Roger Maris captured the single season home run record in 1961, which was shattered by Mark McGwire[59] in 1998, and then Barry Bonds[60] in 2001. There were few records in baseball held in such high regard as 61. Some of those include Lou Gehrig's 2,130 consecutive-games played streak, which was set in 1939, and eclipsed by Cal Ripkin in 1995, and the career home run record of Hank Aaron in 1976 (755), which Barry Bonds broke in 2007.[61] Every player listed is considered *great*, and depending on one's stance on the Hall of Fame and the steroids era, every one of those players belong, without question, in the Hall of Fame, except Roger Maris.

Roger Maris is not in the Hall of Fame. He's never been seriously considered for the Hall of Fame, and he likely never will. Roger Maris was great for one season, but the rest of his career was merely good.

In sports, a greater percentage of what you accomplish has to be great in order to be considered *great*. In the entertainment industry there are numerous examples of a greatness quotient. Harrison Ford, Tom Hanks, and Tom Cruise are three prime examples. I will accept no argument to the contrary. By any measurable standard e.g., box office, awards, critical acclaim, these three actors are great.

Of the top 100 grossing movies in the U.S., 65 of them are from 2001 to 2009, which is such a disproportionate amount that I discounted all films released after 2000 for the purposes of this tally.

A quick search of imdb.com shows that of the top 100 grossing films through the year 2000, Ford, Cruise, and Hanks appeared in 22 of them. But box office isn't enough. How about award recognition?

---

[59] Read: Steroids

[60] Read: Steroids

[61] Read: Steroids

120

Harrison Ford has been nominated for one Academy Award for Best Actor for his role in *Witness* and four Golden Globes for *Witness, The Fugitive, Sabrina,* and *The Mosquito Coast.*

Tom Cruise has been nominated for three Academy Awards; Best Supporting Actor for *Magnolia,* and Best Actor for *Jerry McGuire* and *Born on the Fourth of July.* He was nominated for seven Golden Globes for *Tropic Thunder, Last Samurai, Magnolia, Jerry McGuire, A Few Good Men, Born on the Fourth of July,* and *Risky Business* with wins for *Magnolia, Jerry McGuire,* and *Born on the Fourth of July.*

Tom Hanks has been nominated for Best Actor at the Academy Awards for his roles in *Cast Away, Saving Private Ryan, Forrest Gump, Philadelphia,* and *Big,* with back-to-back wins for *Forrest Gump* and *Philadelphia.* He was nominated for seven Golden Globes for *Charlie Wilson's War, Cast Away, Saving Private Ryan, Philadelphia, Forrest Gump, Sleepless in Seattle,* and *Big* with wins for *Forrest Gump, Cast Away, Philadelphia,* and *Big.*

If awards don't get it done for you, let's add one last piece to the puzzle, critical acclaim. Ford has starred or appeared in 11 movies with over 85 percent positive reviews, according to rottentomoatoes.com. Hanks has appeared in 10, and Cruise has been in seven. Movies of theirs that fell just short of the 85 percent cut off were *A League of Their Own, Philadelphia, Sleepless in Seattle, Road to Perdition, Charlie Wilson's War, A Few Good Men, The Firm, Jerry McGuire, Magnolia, Narc, Tropic Thunder, Return of the Jedi, Indiana Jones and Temple of Doom, Working Girl, Patriot Games, and Clear and Present Danger.*

Can we all agree on *greatness* at this point? Good.

On the flip side of all that *greatness,* Ford has appeared in 13 movies with less than 60 percent positive reviews, Cruise has 16, Tom Hanks has 21.

These three actors are undeniably *great*, but they have each had some seriously bad movies and a big chunk of mediocre films, but we don't think of *Joe vs. The Volcano*, *Random Hearts*, *or Losin' It* when we think of them. We think of *Indiana Jones*, *Big*, and *Top Gun*. We are willing, perhaps even eager to forgive mediocrity in the face of *greatness*. We'll even forgive couch-jumping craziness.

In sports we recognize *greatness*, but it's harder to achieve, and once achieved, we still like to point out the warts.

Dan Marino is widely considered to be one of the *greatest* quarterbacks of all time, but the over-under on how long it will take from the point you hear him mentioned in this conversation until you hear, "Never won the Superbowl" is two sentences.

In 2008, the New York Giants upset the 17-0 New England Patriots in the Superbowl, completing a great six game stretch and putting an end to what had been an unstoppable team in an unbelievable season. You can live the rest of your life and not hear anyone outside the New York metropolitan area refer to the 2007 Giants as a *great* team. If the Patriots had completed that undefeated season they would be considered one of the *greatest* teams of all time, but they fell one game short, so they won't be near the top of anyone's list of *greatest* teams. The difference between the Patriots being *great* and them just being another team that lost in the Superbowl comes down to a broken play and a receiver bringing down a catch with one hand and his helmet.

That's the margin for *greatness* in sports.

Three games through our 4-0 stretch to open Big Ten play, with a 3-0 record over Iowa, Michigan, and Illinois, Sampson was unhappy with that standard. Prior to the Minnesota game Sampson told Don Fischer, "We live in an imperfect world, yet we expect our basketball teams to be perfect" during *The I'm Contractually Obligated to Suffer Through This Once a Week, But I Can't Believe I Agreed to Do This In Front Of A Bunch Of Students Inside Indiana Basketball Coach's Show.*

Sampson was right.[62] We, as sports fans, as Hoosiers, have unrealistic expectations. When I was growing up we won three titles before my 13th birthday. I expected a lot of things. We won a title in 1976, then five years later in 1981. Both of these titles were won in Philadelphia. We won again six years later in 1987, this time in New Orleans. The NCAA Final Four was held in New Orleans again in 1993, six years later. I expected us to go there and win again. I didn't expect this because we were a great team in 1993. I held this expectation in 1988. I believed it because it fit the pattern.

As it turned out we did have a great team in 1993. We spent much of that season as the number one team in the nation. We were the number one seed that year and people less biased than I had every expectation that we would reach the Final Four and bring home a championship.

Through a 31 game regular season we were 28-3 with neutral site losses to Kansas and Kentucky at the beginning of the season, and a tough road loss to Ohio State toward the end of the season. We had a chance to avenge the early season loss to Kansas in the Elite Eight, the way we avenged the early season loss to UCLA in 1992 to reach the Final Four and be jobbed by Ted Valentine in a loss to Duke that would have hurt more had I not expected us to right that wrong in 1993. It was the

---

[62] I know. It hurts me to write that as much as it hurts you to read it.

1975 loss to Kentucky followed by the 1976 undefeated championship run pattern all over again.

But, in practice on Friday, February 19, the ghost of Scott May struck Alan Henderson. Just days before our game against Purdue, Alan Henderson injured his knee after coming down with a pass "kind of spread eagle," according to Knight, casting doubt on the championship prospects for the number one team in the nation. Despite Henderson's injury the team bounced back well from that setback, finished the last few weeks of the season strong, and advanced from the number one seed to the regional finals, but not before more injuries. In the regional semifinal against Louisville, Henderson's freshman classmate, Brian Evans, broke his thumb on his non-shooting hand.

Henderson tried to return to play against Kansas, just as Scott May did in 1975, but as with May, Henderson was nowhere near full strength and only managed to play three minutes in the game. Kansas shot an unthinkable 68 percent in the second half and managed to hold off every run we made, preventing us from making it back to New Orleans to fulfill the pattern that I was certain would hold.

I'm still mad about that Kansas loss. That was our year. Multiple patterns said so. The 1975-1976 pattern, the roughly every five year pattern, the repeating championships in the same cities pattern, it was all there. Plus, we were a great team. Sadly, the pattern that held was one I had never considered. The star returning from injury less than 100 percent and us losing in the biggest game of the season pattern.

Another pattern that I expect to hold is that Louisville won the Championship in 1980 and 1986. We followed each of those championships with one of our own. So, I cheer for Louisville to win the title every year because I know when they do, we'll win the next year.

Are my expectations unrealistic? Absolutely. Are they based on nothing but my misunderstanding of fractals? Possibly. But you know what? I don't care. You know who else had unrealistic expectations? Kelvin Sampson when he expected IU fans to accept anything less than perfection.

With a team led by DJ and EJ, with supporting talent like Bassett and Crawford and a record of 15-1 (4-0) in the Big Ten you're damn right we expected perfection, but, while the record after the first four Big Ten games was perfect, the play that lead to that record was far from it. And we all knew it. So did Sampson.

In the Big Ten opener at Iowa I expected a pretty convincing win. This expectation was well thought out and grounded in an objective appraisal of these two teams and their abilities. These are the factors I considered: We'd had a season of up and down play, Big Ten road games are always a challenge, and we'd spent December playing much lesser competition. But the Sampson Syllogism holds. Wins = good play. And we had won all of our games except the only one against a good team.

Iowa was playing for a first-year coach with a lower level of talent than they otherwise would have. We were the better team and should have won this game by double digits. I tried to be rational, but I wasn't. I complained about the various shortcomings of this team and my frustrations about our coach. My perception of this team and their abilities was clear and accurate. But clear, accurate, rational perception didn't factor into my expectations.

My expectations for this season had not changed. I still expected a Big Ten title and a Final Four run. The talent was there and if playing through adversity (largely off the court and self-inflicted, but adversity nonetheless) helps build character, by the end of the season this team could be exactly what I always expected them to be.

At halftime, stupid reality was beating my ridiculous expectations. And Iowa was very nearly beating my Hoosiers. Iowa had played really well and hit 5-12 from three-point range. It took a Jamarcus Ellis jump shot with three seconds to go to tie the game 34-34 after a tough back-and-forth half.

Iowa started the second half strong, heading into the under 16 minute timeout with a four-point lead. The next 10 minutes were characterized by a lack of restraint on our part, foul trouble, and poor shooting by both teams. We pushed the lead to nine just to have Iowa chop away and get it back to three.

We then went on an 11-1 run over the next 4:30. The 8-0, 1:44 second run that started that spurt consisted of two free throws by EJ, two defensive rebounds by DJ that lead to two DJ dunks at the other end, and capped by EJ grabbing a defensive rebound, which he turned into a fast break layup six seconds later. A Cyrus Tate free throw for Iowa was all they could muster before Crawford grabbed a rebound off his own missed shot and followed it up with a layup. EJ made 1-2 from the line to give us a 13-point lead with 2:10 left to play.

It was a run typical of this team. Thirty-four minutes of up and down play, then a four-minute spurt to add some distance and seal the win. That run should have done it. It should have sealed the game. But this wasn't a preconference game against Chicago State. This was a Big Ten road game.

With IU up 70-57 and the game seemingly out of reach, Justin Johnson found himself isolated on the wing against Ellis and pulled up for a contested three-pointer with 1:56 on the clock. It dropped to make it a

10 point game. Nothing to worry about. Johnson fouled Ellis on the next trip down the court and he went 1-2 from the free throw line to push the lead to 11.

On the next Iowa possession, our defensive rebounding was once again problematic. Tony Freeman pulled up for a 26-foot contested three-pointer, but Seth Gorney grabbed the rebound and Iowa passed the ball around the horn while we gave chase until backup guard Jeff Peterson fired a wide open 12-foot jump-shot from the wing that caught just enough rim to make the rebound difficult. Ellis was left with the option to let go out of bounds off him or try to throw it off an Iowa player. He chose option three, which was to throw it back inbounds to Gorney who kicked the ball out to the top of the key. The ball made it immediately into Johnson's hands and he fired up a three-pointer over a double team of DJ and EJ that went in, cutting the lead to eight with just over one minute to go.

Crawford made two free throws to push the lead back to 10. Ellis blocked a layup attempt, but the ball made its way out to Johnson on the wing, who hit the three while being fouled by AJ Ratliff, resulting in a four-point play and a six-point game with 42 seconds.

Johnson had scored 10 points in 1:12. The game should have been over, but poor rebounding and an insane shooting streak had made it competitive again. Two IU free throws and 21 seconds later, Johnson brought the ball across half court and with eight of the 10 players on the court crammed in the area just to the left of the circle, Johnson pulled up from 30 feet out and hit another three-pointer to cut it five. DJ made two free throws, and then Johnson caught the ball off a screen on the right side of the court and cut it to four with another three.

Iowa put DJ back on the line where he went 1-2 to make the score

78-73 with 12 seconds to play. For the fifth time since the two minute mark, I thought that would just about do it. But I forgot that Justin Johnson doesn't miss three-pointers from anywhere.

Johnson picked up a loose ball, turned, and banked in a three-pointer from one foot inside half court to cut the lead to two with six seconds left to play. Stemler went 1-2 from the line and the fact that Todd Lickliter had to call three timeouts in the first half came back to bite them, as they were out of timeouts and had to go the length of the court with three seconds to play and try to hit another three. Thankfully, Johnson didn't have a chance to take a seventh three-pointer, because it most certainly would have gone in. We escaped Iowa City with a 79-76 win.

Sampson went into the press conference and wanted to talk about the 12 minute stretch in the second half where we played well and ignore the other 28 minutes of the game. See, my belief in patterns is not completely crazy. This one had held all season.

It's hard for fans to do that. I couldn't. I kept thinking, what if we had blocked out down the stretch or made all of our free throws? What would have happened if Lickliter had held back a time out? We got the win, but I was left wanting more. Sampson seemed satisfied. Wins = good.

The Michigan game that followed was less stressful at the end, but the 14-point win came in much the same way many of our other wins did. We played up and down for most of the game, but put together a stretch of good play to put the game out of reach.

This time it was an eight minute stretch to start the second half that did the trick for us. We pushed a six-point halftime lead to 22. Michigan made a little dent in that lead as the game wound down, but this outcome was much better than the Iowa game, and there was less to be critical about. A 14-point road win is nothing to sneeze at. I was starting to feel a little bit better, but I still wasn't convinced and I was right to feel that way.

Illinois came to Assembly Hall next and we played the first half roughly the same way we'd played it for the last two games. It was back and forth, it was close, and we went into the half down by four.

We held our run back for a little longer than we had against Michigan. We spotted them a seven-point lead before making our patented second half run. We went on an 11-2 run over six minutes that started with some EJ free throws with 13:16 to go and ended with a DJ layup with 7:08 on the clock that turned a seven-point deficit into a four-point lead. In between those points there was a nearly three minute stretch where neither team scored. We held on with our fingernails to that four-point lead and limped off our home court.

Illinois was 8-8 overall with an 0-3 Big Ten record heading into that game, which was our first home game in conference against a team that kind of hated us because of EJ's commitment to, then de-commitment from, Illinois. As a team, we couldn't get fired up enough to start this game with anywhere near the same level of passion as our opponent. Thank God Illinois didn't play 12 hours prior to the game and sleep on the bus on the way to Bloomington. We might have been in real trouble.

It was at this point, following three games that were won on the strength of roughly 28 minutes of good play, that Sampson bemoaned our desire for perfection in this, an imperfect world.

Hadn't we learned by now that a win = good play? We were such assholes.

How does one answer those unrealistic expectations? "By going to Minnesota and turning the ball over 26 times and backing into a five point victory?" I hear you saying. Exactly!

Our record was great, but our play was far from it. We did a number of things well against Minnesota. You have to in order to overcome 26 turnovers and win on the road. We shot 86 percent from the line, out-rebounded them by 18, and held them below 40 percent shooting. But doing enough to overcome one awful aspect of your game doesn't make one great. It's like war that way.

An average of eight great minutes a game and a 15-1 record against largely subpar competition doesn't make a team great. And this was a team that should have been *great*. It was a team we all needed to be *great*. We hadn't had talent like this in a few years and, while the record should have had me excited, our play made me nervous.

Elvis reminded us of how *great* he could be in December 1968, but he followed that up by nine years of drug use, weight gain, and Las Vegas lounge acts. In the entertainment world, you can be great less than half the time and still be considered *great*.

In sports it doesn't work that way. A team that is only great for 40 percent of their playing time is a team in trouble, regardless of their record.

We have higher expectations of our favorite sports teams. And we should, because despite what Sampson thinks, winning $\neq$ good and losing $\neq$ bad. It's much more nuanced than that.

Interlude Seven: Expectations

When I was an undergrad, I was a Resident Assistant in the dorms. We used to have meetings every week in our supervisor's room and she always had a jar of peanut M&Ms on her desk. I would walk in, grab a handful, toss them in my mouth, and enjoy the chocolaty goodness. One day, around Christmas, her jar was filled with the red and green holiday assortment. I grabbed my usual handful, threw them in my mouth, and bit down … on mints.

It was disgusting. I had to run to the water fountain to wash the taste out of my mouth, all because I *expected* them to be M&Ms. They were perfectly fine mints, but as I wasn't *expecting* mints, my reaction was severe and negative. If I expected them to be mints I would have been delighted.

I worked with a woman once who, again around Christmas, got a gift from a student. It was a piece of white chocolate with a raspberry center. It was homemade and in the shape of a flower. She had missed lunch, was famished, and had about two minutes to eat so she ran into the teachers' lounge and took a huge bite.

It was soap.

She tried to wash her mouth out, but the water just made the soap turn into foam and bubbles. It took a good five minutes to get it all out of her mouth. Unlike with the mints, there's no way she would have enjoyed eating the soap,[63] even if she knew it was soap, but if she hadn't expected to be given chocolate by her student (which is what most teachers get

---

[63] Over the years she had become quite the connoisseur of soap. Her personal preference was for Lux, but she found that Palmolive had a nice, piquant after-dinner flavor, but Life Boy… YECCH.

from most students) she would not have tried to eat it.

Expectations are crucial to more than just food and Christmas stories, though if you would like to see it in effect around Christmas again, I suggest you watch *Love Actually* and pay attention to the scene where Emma Thompson opens her Christmas present from Alan Rickman.

Consider this scenario: You take a final exam. You leave the class feeling like you nailed it. You feel confident about your responses and are sure you got an A. You get the test back and you got a C. How upset are you? Now, think of the same situation, only you thought you bombed it. How happy are you with that same grade?

Recall when the Arizona Cardinals lost to the Chicago Bears during the 2006 season and Cardinals coach, Dennis Green, went off in the press conference after the game, saying "They are who we thought they were!" repeatedly before hitting the microphone and storming out? Do you know why he was so mad? You guessed it. Expectations.

He knew what to expect from the Bears, game planned accordingly, and expected to win. He was right about what to expect from the Bears, but he still lost. If he knew what to expect from the Bears and was wrong, he would have been surprised. If he had known what to expect from the Bears and expected that his team wouldn't be able to match up, the loss would not have bothered him as much as it did. His expectations informed his reaction.

Just as my expectations, justified or not, rational or not, influenced how I reacted to this team, and every other IU team I've ever watched. I'm still mad at the 1993 Kansas Jayhawks because I expected us to win the NCAA Championship. If I'd have thought we were going to lose, I'd have been upset. I hate it when we lose, but I wouldn't still be mad about it 15 years later.

Chapter Eight: Comeuppance

I am preparing a pitch for a major TV network. Tell me what you think. I want to do a remake... no. Stop. Scratch that. Remakes are for cheesy television shows that are turned into cheesier movies. I want to do a re-imagining. Those seem to be all the rage with the kids today. First there was the stellar frakking success that was *Battlestar Galactica*, which spawned a number of not so good re-imaginings. *Flash Gordon, Bionic Woman, Knight Rider,* I'm looking in your direction. Then there was *Star Trek*, which took all the things you loved about *Star Trek* and did the unthinkable; made them exciting and fun.

What I'm proposing is this: A re-imagining of *Gilligan's Island.* The same basic themes stay in place. A group of people, stranded on a deserted island, modern conveniences made out of coconut shells, an amazing ability for guest stars to show up on the island, etc., but I want to make two pretty significant changes: First, I want to replace the group of strangers from different walks of life with an entire college basketball team. So, instead of it being a story about strangers being forced to coexist with one another, it becomes a story about a group of people who are supposed to know how to work together, being forced to work together in a strange environment, like a Big Ten road game, for instance.

The second change I want to make is that instead of one character, Gilligan, doing something incredibly stupid that ruins everyone's chances of getting off the island every week, the entire group fights off injuries and suspensions and conspires, subconsciously, to do something incredibly stupid, but somehow, week after week, they make it off the island, only to find themselves marooned on a different island the next week.

I've prepared an extensive show bible that takes the show through five full seasons. And the beauty of the thing is that somewhere in the middle of the third season, when it's clear I need to shake some things up to bring in new viewers (a la Syndey Bristo taking down SD-6 right after the Superbowl or Jack's flashbacks actually being a flash forward to after they made it off the island in the Season 3 finale of *Lost*, or anytime a cuter, younger kid is brought in because the other cute young kids aren't as young or cute as they used to be) there's going to be a fundamental shift in the show.

The entire team will continue to get injured, suspended, and behave in the most ridiculous ways imaginable, only now they will find that their behavior has suddenly made it impossible to get off the island.

A twist like that, aside from making M. Night Shyamalan envious, would have an impact on both the members of the team stuck on the island and on the fans of the show. The characters would be forced to face adversity beyond that which they had faced previously and either rise to meet the challenge or wilt in the face of it. The audience would be put

135

in a very uncomfortable position.

After three years of knowing what to expect from their favorite show, they would no longer be able to count on a positive outcome at the end of all the struggle they are watching. Think Radar coming into the O.R. and reading the telegram that Lt. Col. Henry Blake's helicopter had been shot down and all aboard killed after he had been discharged and was on his way home in the third season finale of M*A*S*H.

I'm sure there will be a certain level of outrage. Letters will be written to the local papers, bloggers will write scathing reviews of the show and proclaim that I have jumped the shark, message boards will be filled with anger, #freegilligan will trend, but people will keep tuning in hoping to see the team finally escape the island and make it home.

Does that not sound like the best idea ever? The beauty part is that I already have the entire cast and a writer who can't imagine things going any better if he had written it himself.

After the Minnesota clusterfrak we headed home for two conference games that upheld the story arc of the first 15 games. Poor play for a while, good play for a while, and a victorious finish with a respectable margin.

Our home stand began against Penn State, a game that held exactly to that form. The second half run began a little later, but the result was the same. We defeated a short-handed Penn State squad, 81-65, whose leading scorer, Speedy Claxton, was lost for the season with a knee injury in their previous game against Wisconsin. But when Iowa entered Assembly Hall for a rematch that had been, literally, days in the making, they entered like George Harrison pulled into a talent agent's office.

We played well against Iowa from the start; we stopped Johnson from scoring 30 points in a three-minute stretch, we started our run in the first half and carried it over into the second half. We pushed the halftime lead of 11 to a final score of 65-43. Overall, we improved over our previous performance against Iowa in just about every way possible.

Was this an early clue to the new direction, or were the Hawkeyes just troublemakers?

Could this be the turnaround in play that I had been waiting for? We were as full strength as we were going to get. After his semester in exile, A. J. Ratliff had returned, gotten injured, and then returned again in good health to come off the bench and contribute. We had played our first home and home and shown improved play from the first game to the second. We were 17-1 (6-0).

Then Olivia showed up to out-cute Rudy. Our next game was the inexplicable nonconference game stuck in the middle of the conference season. I hate these games. They don't help your goal of winning the Big Ten and frequently do more harm than good.

In February, 2002 with IU in the middle of a tough battle for the Big Ten title we took a break from Big Ten play to square off against Louisville. I wish we played Louisville every year, just as we play Kentucky, but not in the middle of the conference season. Against Louisville that year we played a tough game against a good team and beat them by 15, seemingly helping our chances for a better NCAA seed and preparing us for the type of teams we would play in March.

But a win isn't all we got out of this game. We also got the chance to let our bench shine for the final six games of the regular season, as star forward Jared Jeffries twisted his ankle in the game. He missed the next game against Wisconsin, a loss that tightened the Big Ten race considerably. Jeffries returned in the next game, but wasn't 100 percent for the rest of the conference season. Jeffries injury and limited mobility hurt his performance and the team's by extension. We went 3-3 over the final six conference games, including the loss at home to Wisconsin, costing us an outright Big Ten title. Instead, our lone Big Ten title of the decade came as part of a four way tie at 11-5.

The team battled through the NCAA tournament before losing to Maryland in the championship game, but the injury to Jeffries effectively scuttled our Big Ten title hopes, and it wouldn't have happened had we not stepped outside of our conference schedule to play a made-for-TV game against Louisville.

We weren't the only ones scheduling like this, which seemed to be all the reason Coach Sampson needed to make scheduling decisions, but playing these games does two things I don't like. First, it takes your attention away from what should be your priority, conference games. The goal is, and has got to be, to win the Big Ten. Playing UConn at this point doesn't help that. On the contrary, shoving another game in there actually dulls the focus the team had on the task at hand.

Secondly, let's assume we have the worst-non-injury-case-scenario and lose this game. Then you have to shift your focus back to your important games with a loss hanging over your head. Now let's go even further down the worst-case-scenario trail. What if you follow a tough nonconference game with a tough conference road game at, I don't know, let's say Wisconsin, and you lose that game too, which isn't out of the realm of possibility as nearly everyone who traveled to Wisconsin in the 00s came away with a loss. You go from having a team that is undefeated in conference on a winning streak to a team that has lost two in a row in the heart of conference season. It doesn't mean you are a worse team than

138

you were before, but it does change perception and it may change the team's attitude.

In other words, you might have the same group of guys acting the same way they did before and suddenly find themselves unable to get off the island.

It's very difficult to change someone else's behavior under ideal circumstances, but it is much more difficult to change someone else's behavior once they have had a great deal of success doing things the wrong way, and 17-1 (6-0) is a lot of success playing mediocre basketball. Back-to-back losses at this point in the season would be very hard to overcome.

So, why play these games? It bolsters your nonconference schedule a little bit in the eyes of the NCAA committee. But let's be honest about this. If you get rid of this game, focus on the title, win the Big Ten title, and finish the conference season with two or three losses, in a normal year, that puts you at a number one or number two seed, so this game only helps if you win it, but happen to falter later. But Memphis's strength of schedule didn't keep them out of the number one seed when they finished the season with one loss.[64]

The other reason to play these games is money. A nationally televised home game brings in a lot of money and exposure, though, if we played UConn in December instead of one of the cream puffs we did play, we would have gotten the same national spotlight, exposure, and attention, which brings me back to finding no good reason to play these games at this time.

---

[64] This never happened. Thanks to Derrick Rose and John Calipari.

We got off to a great start against UConn, jumping out to a quick 9-0 lead on the power of three-pointers from EJ, Ellis, and Bassett, but, UConn, without its two best players, who were suspended just prior to the game, came back to take a five point half-time lead.

After our early three-point shooting success we had one of the worst shooting days I've ever seen. We went 0-9 over a six minute stretch in the first half, finishing the half shooting a woeful 8-27 from the field for 29.6 percent.

Not only were we shooting horribly, we were getting beat on the boards 22-16 while UConn shot 12-26 for a much more respectable 46 percent. This felt a lot like Seasons 1-3, and there was no reason at all to assume that we wouldn't find our four-to-six minute stretch of good play and put UConn behind us, probably around the 12 minute mark. Except this is what we like to call a paradigm shift and that run never came. We finished the game shooting 37 percent to UConn's 43 percent. We were out-rebounded by 15 and never really seemed in the game in the second half.

But even when you turn things on their ears, you have to leave some aspects the same, or the audience won't have anything with which to identify. When Season 4 began, not only did Hawkeye have to welcome in a new Commanding Officer, the horse-loving and cantankerous Sherman Potter, he had to get used to a new bunkmate and best friend, one BJ Hunnicut. But he kept cracking jokes and saving soldiers. Frank continued to be a horse's ass. Klinger kept dressing in drag, trying to get his section 8. Hot Lips kept having the hottest of lips.

DJ was our Captain Benjamin Franklin "Hawkeye" Pierce, notching another double-double with 10 points and 13 rebounds, and Bassett played the role of Captain BJ Hunnicut, scoring 18 points on 6-10

140

shooting, three assists and no turnovers, but it wasn't enough to hold off Hasheem Thabeet and his scrappy band of unranked Huskies. It was exactly like the Xavier game minus that 15 minute break to change the net.

The UConn loss seemed to take something out of Sampson as well. His postgame press conference was filled with the usual praise of the opponent, but he found it difficult to find anything positive to say about the way we played. "You can spin this anyway you want, but the bottom line is, we didn't play well enough to win." And remember loss = played bad.

He was asked to talk about what Crawford brought to the team in the second half, which is exactly the kind of question Sampson should love. It gives him the perfect chance to do what he loves, focus entirely on the good parts of the game. He responded, "I thought Jordan played more under control, didn't turn it over. The first half, for instance—and I haven't seen the film— but the defensive breakdowns should not be tolerated, just unacceptable. We switch most guard-to-guard screens. All you have to do is communicate. Whoever sets the screens, that player's guy is who calls the switch. Two or three occasions the guy comes out the other side and is standing there wide open."

Who is this guy? In one respect I was glad to see him address our inability to defend a ball screen, which we've been bad at since the first game of the season, but he was having real trouble finding anything positive to say. It's one thing for the story to take a "Jack's off the island now, how did that happen?" twist, but when Mulder went from believer to skeptic it threw off the rhythm of the entire show. What would have happened if Hawkeye had gone into a deep depression and quit drinking home-distilled martini's and making jokes and started shooting heroin and nodding all day after Henry died and Trapper went home?

He also had trouble confining his answers to the questions that were asked without getting a little defensive and answering charges that had not been leveled. This is not the same as ignoring the question to stick with your talking points. Embracing your talking points is an effort to control the message. This kind of defensive rambling is a sign of control lost.

He was asked about EJ's game. He said, "Yeah, he looked like he was struggling tonight. The game didn't really come easy to him. It is easy when you see somebody every day to see what is wrong with them. You guys see us every day so it is easy to point out what is wrong with us, but we still have a good team. This is a setback. We still have 12 more games and our team is going to win a ton more games and this may wind up being the best thing that happens to this team."

He said two things that really surprised me. The first was that he found our effort "disgusting," which is a really strong word to use about your own team. That's a word that should be reserved for when football players pretend to moon a crowd of people who frequently, actually moon the opposing team. The other was that he gave up on the "we're a young team" defense. He said, "We have some freshmen, but we're not a young team." I know Sampson's self-contradictions shouldn't have shocked me at this point, but this direct policy reversal was startling. It sounded like he was honestly out of excuses that he could use that would convince him or us that God was in his heaven and all was right with the world.

The measure of both a man and a team is how he/they respond when things don't go the way they want them to go. You can't control everything that happens to you, but you can control how you respond to it. Bad things happen to everyone. It's how you handle them that determines who you are.

The 2002 team, while struggling mightily down the stretch, managed to do enough to tie for the conference title and upset number one Duke in the regional semifinals, and then plowed through the rest of their competition to make it all the way to the NCAA title game. Whether this team had that kind of character remained to be seen.

After the UConn loss a number of people started to see that maybe this particular emperor was walking down the street in his skivvies and began to say so out loud. The team left the floor to a smattering of boos for their subpar effort. Message boards were suddenly filled with Hennies and Pennies, all proclaiming different dates for the fall of the sky. I didn't feel great about our performance against UConn, hell, I hadn't felt great about many of our performances to this point, but I never stopped expecting us to win the next game, right the ship, and get off the island. This wasn't our first loss of the season and probably wouldn't be our last, but we were 17-2 (6-0), tied for first in the Big Ten with a game against Wisconsin coming up that would allow us to put some breathing room between ourselves and Wisconsin, Purdue, and Michigan State. The Big Ten had already started to settle into a four-team race and any games against these three schools would be critical to our title hopes.

Many people were beginning to feel that we wouldn't reach our goal on account of our ob-stac-les, as witnessed by the boos, the editorials, and the message boards. I, however, still thought we had a pretty good chance because as we've seen, I was incapable of expecting anything other than a win. I had so bought into the narrative of the first three seasons that a switch from flashbacks to flash-forwards was not a part of my worldview.

As much as I'd like to lay this on the playing of a nonconference game in the middle of the conference season, I just can't make that stretch, but in practice prior to the Wisconsin game, EJ got hurt again. He injured his left hand, though it was his non-shooting hand, so he wouldn't be missing any games, but he would be playing with a brace. I was about ready to take off my hat and hit someone over the head with it.

Holman was out for the year, Bassett had an injury that was not going to heal by the end of the season, and EJ would have to play with a brace on his left hand. Crawford and Bassett had both been suspended for three games earlier in the year and AJ spent a semester getting his grades in order, and then hurt himself upon his return. That sounds like the description of a team of castaways well positioned to get off the island and make it all the way home, does it not?

The Wisconsin game that followed was another ugly game, our third truly ugly game out of the last five, with UConn and Minnesota being the *Phantom Menace* and *Attack of the Clones* to this *Revenge of the Sith*.

Our shooting did not improve from the UConn game. We actually shot worse, 33.3 percent to Wisconsin's shiny 34.5 percent. Neither team could make a three-pointer. We were a dismal 14.3 percent on 3-21 shooting. We also turned the ball over 12 times to their six.

EJ's wrist injury seemed to impact his play. He shot 2-7 from three and only got to the line twice. His injured hand made it much tougher for him to drive the lane effectively.

DJ was stellar. He has the only Hoosier to shoot over 50 percent from the field. He was the only player not named Eric Gordon to shoot a free throw. His 8-10 from the line and 7-13 from the field netted him 22 points to go along with his 17 rebounds. But DJ being the man was not nearly enough to overcome a 1-7 night from Bassett and a 0-4 performance from Crawford, and we came up 13 points short against a tough Wisconsin team on the road.

144

If looked at objectively, which isn't really my strong suit, this was not likely to be a win for us under the best of circumstances, but it came immediately following a poor performance and loss to an out-of-league opponent and we played poorly the entire game. For the second game in a row there was no second half spurt to put us in the driver's seat. Two bad losses in a row had left a bad taste in my mouth.

To make it that much worse, there was very little new about these two games. We played the same kind of ball we'd been playing, but as with Xavier, we tried to play it against good teams and we ended up on the losing end each time.

Two things could have happened after this two game stretch: The team could see the error of their ways, stop making the same mistakes over and over again and get off the island once and for all, or they could view their task as suddenly insurmountable, stop trying to get off the island all together and start working on real breakthroughs in coconut technology.

With the heart of the Big Ten season coming up and a loss to one of the other three teams realistically fighting for the title, the trial by fire was just beginning. And his team was about to be tested in ways they could not have foreseen.

So was every Hoosier fan.

Interlude Eight: The Walk On

As a boy, I dreamed of growing up and playing basketball for Coach Knight at Indiana. It never occurred to me that this dream was unrealistic until no one was recruiting me to do anything at all by my junior year of high school, including the varsity boys' basketball coach at my high school. It seems there is very little call for a 6'2 power forward who can't jump, dribble, or shoot reliably from farther than six feet out.

I viewed sports, basketball in particular, as something to do for fun. I loved to play and I loved to watch, but I never thought that I could become a better basketball player by working at it for hours. When practice was over I went home and did other things. When the season was over, I played something else.

I went to summer camps at the high school when I was in grade school, but I never went to a camp at a college. That seemed like something that was reserved for people who were better than me already, not people who were working to be better.

It's possible that this is just part of my personality. I never gave much thought to how much one had to work at something to be great at it. One of the reasons that I never gave it much thought was that I never saw anyone work their way up from nothing to succeed at that level before. *Rudy* didn't come out until late in my high school career and it was about football, so I didn't see it until well after that. Besides, I didn't really want to play college basketball. I wanted to play for Indiana. And my understanding of how that worked was as follows:

You are a star for your high school team.

You win the state championship.

You go to Indiana.

Eventually you win the National Championship.

I knew you got a scholarship to play college basketball. I didn't know there were walk-ons. I'm sure I could name some walk-ons from when I was a kid, but I didn't know they existed. To my knowledge, everyone on IU's team was the star of their high school team who had won the state title their senior year.

This all changed in 2003-2004.

The first time I became aware of the walk-on phenomenon was when Ryan Tapak, local boy done good, cracked the starting lineup for five games. It was a great story. He was an inspiration for everyone who was too small to play Division I basketball and had never seen *Rudy*. If you worked hard enough you could start for IU. Then he graduated and handed the reins to Errek Suhr who was even smaller than Tapak (5'9 to Tapak's 6'2) and was even more local (Bloomington to Tapak's Indianapolis). Suhr started four games his senior season.

In 2007-2008 I became a big fan of Kyle Taber, the latest walk-on to earn a scholarship and get some time in the starting lineup. Taber actually started one game in 2006-2007 and by the end of the 2007-2008 season he had started four.

Then I realized something. The reason I never knew anything about any walk-ons for IU was that walk-ons don't earn scholarships and work their way into the starting lineup. Ninety percent of the time when that does happen, it means the team is not very good.[65] And IU was very good when I was growing up

[65] Packer Method

The 2003-2004 season, when Tapak breached the starting lineup, we finished 14-15 and didn't make it into any postseason tournament. The next two seasons, Mike Davis' last and Sampson's first, were transitional seasons full of ups and downs. The teams were better than the 2003-2004 squad, but the reliance on walk-on and former walk-on talent was a sure sign that things were not as they should have been.

When Taber entered the game at the 8:14 mark of the win over Northwestern that followed the back-to-back losses to UConn and Wisconsin, while Mike White and The Giant spent most of the game on the bench, I should have seen it for what it was; a sign that something was rotten in Denmark.

A team does not look to tap the walk-on talent unless there are serious problems. As much as I love to see these kids succeed and be rewarded for all their hard work, as much as I cheer for them when they hit the floor and pull for them to succeed, I know, in the back of my mind, that it is not a good sign.

When you don't have enough players who you have spent time recruiting and deemed worthy to offer scholarships and you have to look for help from the guys you brought on to be bodies in practice, the canary has come up from the coal mine, and if you hadn't nailed his feet to the perch, he'd be pushing up the daisies.

Beware of the walk-on.

Chapter Nine: The Opposite of Love

Let's talk about love for a moment, shall we? Or rather, the opposite of love. The dictionary in the guts of my computer defines love as "an intense feeling of deep affection." Sounds about right, but perhaps a bit overly simplistic. I can't imagine that all of the world's great poetry and 90 percent of the world's great pop songs (the rest were written about cars, surfing, transvestites, or how much Don McLean hates Mick Jagger) were written about something so simplistic as an intense feeling of deep affection.

The definition of hate that my computer-guts dictionary gives me is to "feel intense or passionate dislike for." Affection and dislike are pretty much opposites, but beyond that, these two things have a lot in common. The words "feel" and "intense" play a prominent role in both of these emotions. Love and hate are two sides of the same coin. How many times have you seen prisoners with "love" tattooed on one set knuckles and "hate" tattooed on the other set? Yeah, me either, but I chalk that up to largely not spending a lot of time with prisoners. If movies are any indication (and when are movies not an indication) this is as common as "Mom" tattooed on an arm or boobs tattooed on a back.

Elie Wiesel very famously said, "The opposite of love is not hate. It is indifference." This feels very true to me. How many times have you seen a movie where a guy has "Love" tattooed on one set of knuckles and "Meh" tattooed on the other?

Computer-guts dictionary defines indifference as "lack of interest, concern or sympathy." Lack of something and intense and passionate something are not opposite sides of the same coin. One is on a coin, the other is an otter. Very far removed from one another.

There have been many great lovers written about over time and many more portrayed in movies and television. You've got Don Juan, Romeo, Cassanova, and Arthur Fonzarelli, but each of these characters were deeply flawed. Don Juan frequently ended up in hell after dinner engagements with ghosts. Romeo was a dope who should have never bought poison. If Casanova was so great, how come he's dead? Arthur Fonzarelli was in his thirties, lived above a garage, and dated high school girls. They all have one other thing in common which limits their use for the purpose of our discussion here, which is they only loved other people.

There really is only one perfect example of the lover. One man who, if he finds something even a little bit pleasing, loves it with a fiery passion that could ignite, let's say, a giant pile of tires. And one man who, when he dislikes something, hates it with total disregard to reason and does things to intentionally cause real damage to that which he hates. I'm speaking, of course, of Homer J. Simpson.

Let us first examine the many loves of Homer Simpson. He loves all of these things, it would seem, equally and without apology. He loves beer, donuts, his wife, his family, chili cook offs, Aberdeen High School, strangling, mid-season replacements, the XFL, bowling, television, large cup holders, the "workin' overtime part" of *Takin' Care of Business*, Grand Funk Railroad, floor pie, his mother, footballs in the groin, his beer cold, his TV loud, and his homosexuals fa-laming.

Now for things Homer hates. It's a much smaller list. He hates church, Mr. Burns, Ted Koppel (no, wait, he finds him witty and informative), parent-teacher conferences (at least Bart's), Dean Bitterman (hell, just about any college dean), Springfield U or Springfield A&M (he has trouble keeping this straight), and most of all, Ned Flanders.

The Ned Flanders relationship is the most direct proof we have of the close connection between love and hate. For the purposes of this discussion, Flanders is our very own Archaeopteryx.[66]

When Homer accepted a job as the food critic for the *Springfield Shopper* it was an ideal job for him because he got to focus almost exclusively on something he loved, food, and tell people all about it. His reviews were too positive for the cynical and grizzled newspaper man in charge. Homer simply loved too much.

Homer's first review, however, while full of love for the food he ate, was laced with hatred. And misspellings. He made several threatening references to the UN, used words like pascetti and mamatoes, and at the end, in an effort to reach his minimum word count, wrote "screw Flanders" over and over again. Even in the embrace of one of his true loves, he had to express his hatred of Flanders.

When the children of Springfield got themselves stranded in nearby Shelbyville while trying to reacquire the symbol of town pride and the backbone of their economy, the lemon tree, the parents, driven by the love they have for their children (and their hatred of Shelbyvillians) needed an RV they could all use to get to Shelbyville. Homer had one they could use, "Flanderses! Pile in everyone. No time to wipe your feet." Again, even when driven by love, Homer manages to volunteer the use of Flanderses' property, while actively encouraging everyone to destroy it.

And speaking of destruction, consider the events surrounding the big Homecoming game between Springfield U (Homer's "alma mater" as there's really no word for the school at which you only attended one class) and Springfield A&M.

---

[66] BOOOM! 1,000 bonus points if you knew what that was without looking it up. I didn't.

Homer: "And the big game between Springfield U and Springfield A&M. I hate Springfield U so much!"

Lisa: "You went to Springfield U. You hate A&M."

Homer: "So much."

His love for the U (or hate, whichever) leads Homer to build a float for the homecoming parade, which brings Flanders into things, ever so briefly.

Flanders: "Excuse me neighbor. I couldn't help but notice you picked pretty much all of my flowers!"

Homer: "Can't make a float without flowers."

Flanders: "Sure enough. But did you have to salt the earth so nothing would ever grow again?"

Homer: "hehehehehe ... yeah"

Presumably, while getting his supplies to build his float Homer chose that instead of buying flowers he would A.) Steal Flanders', and B.) Buy bags of salt instead. Love = float (and flowers). Hate = Flanders.

We have two examples of Homer acting out of love toward his neighbor: When Flanders' house is destroyed by a hurricane, Homer leads the town in an effort to rebuild Casa Flanders. Sadly, his intentions far outweigh his abilities and what he builds isn't so much a home as it is a fun house that promptly falls over, leading Flanders to insult the entire town for their incompetence and various other shortcomings. He saves his worst for last, "Homer, you are the worst human being I have ever met." Even when Homer acts out of love toward Flanders it leads very quickly to hate.

And finally, there's an episode entitled *Homer Loves Flanders*. In his desire to go to the big, sold out game between Springfield and Shelbyville, who Homer hates by the way, he can just accept Ned's generous offer to accompany him to the game with the tickets he won off the radio, or he can go over to Flanders' house, bash his head in with a lead pipe, and take the tickets. He tries the latter, but is forced to accept the former.

Flanders gave Homer something he wants, and Homer begins to realize Flanders is a pretty great guy after all. But after spending far too much time with him, Flanders begins to hate Homer. In this very intense and complicated relationship love and hate are inextricably linked and often times hard to differentiate.

When I'm looking for some deep, insightful words about the nature of life and love I go to all the usual places. Shakespeare, Elie Wiesel, Bob Dylan, Flavor Flav, and very often the Wacky Weatherman, Harris K. Telemacher, who is the source of this little gem, "Why is it that we don't always recognize the moment when love begins but we always know when it ends?" The same can be said for apathy.

I can't tell you for certain when I first started not giving a shit about Illinois Basketball. I have far too many years logged actively not caring to narrow apathy's origin to one point in time. But I can tell you with pinpoint clarity the moment the Illini faithful registered a blip on my emoto-meter.

On March 5, 1989, I watched our star player and clutchiest of clutch shooters, Jay Edwards, pull up and hit an impossible jump shot from the baseline that seemed to float over the backboard and into the basket to tie the game against Illinois at 67 with two seconds left on the clock. Heading into that game we were 24-5 (14-1) with our sights set on a Big Ten championship after what can best be described as a rocky start to the season. After seven games that season we were 3-4 with losses to Notre Dame, Louisville, North Carolina, and Syracuse, all by double-digits. Against Louisville, North Carolina, and Syracuse we surrendered over 100 points and were largely outclassed.

For 13-year-old me, less than two years removed from the glory of Keith Smart and Steve Alford, I expected IU to be in the championship game every year and to be the Big Ten champion no less frequently. The loss to local rival Louisville was a tough one to argue on the playground, but the complete dismantling by our 1987 championship opponent was particularly hard to watch.

We rebounded from those early season problems to lead the Big Ten with three games left to go. The Illinois game was a battle throughout, and when Jay Edwards hit that jump shot, one of his 45[67] last-second shots in his short two-year career, we had the momentum and another victory in overtime seemed assured.

But then stupid Nick Anderson and his stupid three-pointer went in at the stupid buzzer and we lost at home.

As much as this loss bothered me, and still does to the extent that I remember it really well over 20 years later, it didn't matter. We won the Big Ten that year and made it to the Sweet 16, losing to eventual national runner-up Seton Hall. Illinois made it to the Final Four that year, but as usual they didn't win, so who cares.

That tiny blip on the emoto-meter is the only thing about Illinois to

[67] Packer Method

register for me until February 7, 2008. This was a game on an island. Not in a *Gilligan's Island* meets the Harlem Globetrotters kind of way, but in a the-meaning-of-this-game-is-completely-disconnected-from-everything-else-that-surrounds-it kind of way.

Heading into the game the headlines from around Indiana and Illinois read as follows, "Gordon's snub the rub for Illiini basketball," "The Gordon Game," "Public Enemy #23," "Hell Hath No Fury Like a Student Cheering Section Scorned," "IU's Gordon Must Withstand Illini's Orange Krush," "Expect Illini Hostility," and "Face of the Illini Enemy."

There was no mention made of conference implications, standings, or anything really relating to the game itself. The story going in was EJ committed to Illinois, de-committed then committed to Indiana. Illinois fans are pissed, expect them to act like douche bags.

There was a lot of concern that this would result in EJ being very distracted heading into the game and that it might impact his performance. I didn't share those concerns. EJ seemed to be nonplussed by pretty much everything. In fact, on the ability to handle adverse circumstances scale, EJ seemed to fall much closer to the Colonel Nathan Jessup "I eat breakfast 300 yards away from 4,000 Cubans who are trained to kill me" side than the Lt. Colonel Andrew Markinson "This guy got into full dress uniform, stood in the middle of that room, drew a nickel-plated pistol from his holster and fired a bullet into his mouth" end of the scale.

According to Pat Forde, ESPN senior writer and former *Louisville Courier-Journal* ass-basket,[68] Dakich told EJ prior to the game, "If you're

---

[68] I can't really explain my former dislike for Pat Forde. I think my teenage self disagreed with him once about something he wrote about the long-term prospects for soccer's U.S. popularity and that kind of stuck. He was right, but

going to let a kid in an orange shirt who's an engineering student from Wilmette bother you, you're not as tough as I thought you were."

In other words, HULK UP, BROTHER![69]

The actions of the Illinois players and the fan section prior to and during this game crossed the line from pissed off rival to complete lack of class. You expect a player to get booed and possibly some relatively clever taunts, but you don't expect a player during handshakes to lower his shoulder into his opponent's chest in an attempt to knock him back a step and intimidate him, which is exactly what Illinois guard Chester Frazier did during player introductions.

To my surprise, and maybe I shouldn't have been surprised by this but I was, all of the extraneous stuff seemed to get to EJ during the first half. He started the game out overly aggressive. He took some rushed shots, forced penetration when the openings really weren't there, and finished the half with one point.

If this were just a battle of freshmen we would have been in trouble as Illinois' Demetri McCamey was up on EJ 8-1 in the first half. Sampson was actively recruiting McCamey prior to his decision to attend Illinois and the NCAA and IU subsequently interviewed him in regards to Sampson's own, special, definition of "actively recruiting." Fortunately for us we had more than one freshman and more than one half to play.

Whatever was said to EJ at the half was the right thing because he was a different player in the second half. He scored our first five points of the half, 17 points total, and with 25 seconds in the game and Illinois

I'm still holding on to that one for some reason. Sorry, Pat. Bygones?

[69] Also, screw you Wilmette, and engineering students.

leading by three he scored our final three points of the half on a 25-foot bank-shot that sent the game into overtime.

The first half offensively for IU belonged to DJ and Crawford, who combined for 17 of our 25 points. The first overtime period was not an offensive showcase for anyone, but Crawford was able to reassert himself. He scored our only six points of the period, but that was enough to force a second overtime.

McCamey didn't take any time off. After scoring eight points in the first half he scored 18 in the second half, was responsible for four of the six points in the first overtime, and hit a three-pointer with six seconds left to go in the second overtime to pull Illinois within two.

But McCamey's seven three-pointers were not enough to overcome the free throw shooting inability of Illinois center Shaun Pruitt and the collective performance of the Hoosiers as the second overtime was handed over to Bassett, who put up 11 points in the final five minutes to seal the road win.

Clearly, there was a level of hatred built up by Illinois fans towards us prior to the game, but they never really rated a response on my emoto-meter. I just never cared enough about what Illinois fans thought. Why would I? Aside from one jump shot in 1989 they never did anything to upset or even interest me. To me, it's akin to having a passionate dislike for the prime minister of Canada.

A more accurate description of my relationship to Illinois fans is the relationship between Johnny Snow and Dr. Horrible. Johnny Snow kept trying to challenge the doctor to fight and insisted on calling him his archnemesis. Dr. Horrible hardly cared and was only moderately annoyed that this guy kept trying to inflate the importance of their relationship. For someone of Dr. Horrible's stature, a Johnny Snow was simply not worth the time or energy it would take to hate him.

That's how I was with Illinois prior to this game. Why bother hating Illinois? I had bigger fish to hate. But, the behavior of their fans and of Frazier at the start of the game crossed a line for me. They went from a nonentity to my least favorite team in the Big Ten.

So, I congratulate you Illinois. You've got my attention, which I'm sure was your plan all along. I'm giving you three years to do something interesting to keep my attention, otherwise I'm going back to ignoring you.[70]

After we beat Illinois we traveled to Ohio State where we came away with what I can only describe as the least tense six-point victory I've ever seen. At no point during the game was I nervous about the outcome. We were better than Ohio State and after that game we had a three game stretch against the other three teams fighting for the Big Ten Title, Wisconsin, Michigan State and Purdue. If we were to win those three games we'd be alone at the top and in complete control of our own fate.

---

[70] In the years since, Bruce Weber has said and done enough to help extend my hatred, but then Illinois fired him at the end of the 2012 season, and then offered the job to three people before finding someone who'd take it. Which is just pathetic. So I'm back to not caring about the Illini. Hell, I might even pitty them.

Interlude Nine: Iced Tea

Iced tea can tell you everything you need to know about a person. I knew a man once who had a high profile job. He was extremely successful, seen by many to be the best in his field not only in his time, but of all time. It was a job that people take for years at a time, with signed contracts and everything. It was very official.

This man decided he didn't want to do this job anymore. It had been a long time and it wasn't as much fun as it had once been. He had a successor all lined up, so he resigned. The timing of his decision was a little strange, coming right in the middle of things. On his way out the door, he looked around at all the people who worked for him and said, "If I'm not here in the morning, it's all up to you guys," and they all kind of laughed. "One other thing," he continued, "don't anybody bother that iced tea of mine. When I come back to visit I wanna make damn sure it's where I left it." When he came in the next day to talk to the staff, his iced tea was right where it was supposed to be.

That man was Bob Knight.

Draw from this what you will, but I'll tell you what it says to me. When Bob Knight abruptly resigned from his position as head of men's basketball coach at Texas Tech University in the middle of the 2007-2008 season it caught pretty much everyone by surprise, but it shouldn't have. I'm not saying anyone should have gotten out of bed that morning, rolled over and said, "You know Martha, I wouldn't be a bit surprised if Bob Knight retired today." But the idea that Knight would choose to walk on his own schedule should have surprised no one.

And the story of the iced tea should tell you exactly why. When Myles Brand fired Bob Knight in September 2000, he robbed Knight of what he seems to care most about, control. Knight's entire career was built around the notion that he was in control and that you could "do it my way, or watch your butt."

Knight was not able to leave Indiana under his own terms, so he was sure as hell going to leave Texas Tech that way. He set it up so that his son, Pat, would be his successor. He made sure to grab the spotlight one last time as a coach. He forced everyone to react to him and not the other way around. He quit as he coached, on his terms.

And as one final act of proof in his complete and total control over everything, even things that don't matter, he made sure his iced tea was right where he left it when he came back.

Chapter Ten: Oh, One More Thing

Kelvin Sampson is a cheater and a liar. Those aren't my words, though I agree with them, so much as they represent the opinion of the NCAA. Come with me now. We will take a trip through the events that have brought us to this shameful place.

On September 8, 2000, a disrespectful punk named Kent Harvey, while walking past Bob Knight, who was entering Assembly Hall, called out, "Hey Knight." Coach Knight took this little twerp by the arm and told him that he should have referred to him as Mr. Knight, or Coach Knight.

On September 10, after two days spent dancing the dance of joy wearing naught but a loin cloth and some face paint, Myles Brand proved he was the alpha dog and fired Bob Knight for violating the "zero-tolerance" policy he placed on Knight the previous spring. And on September 12, IU capitulated to the demands of the players and named Mike Davis as the interim head coach.

On March 21, 2001, after completing the season with 21 victories, Davis was named as the head coach and given a four-year contract.

One year to the day later, on March 21, 2002, IU defeated Duke in the Sweet 16. I've watched this game multiple times and I still have no idea how we won. It remains the most gradual comeback I've ever seen. Early during the 2001-2002 season, I told a number of people that Duke's season would end because Jason Williams couldn't shoot free throws. I have never been more right. I also bet a friend in October 2001 that AJ Moye could block a Carlos Boozer lay-up. Sometimes my prescience surprises even me.

On March 23, 2002, Davis' team beat up on Sampson's Oklahoma team in the Final Four. We lost in the championship game to a better Maryland team, but this run secured Davis a six year contract extension. That turned out to be a fantastic decision.

On March 12, 2004, IU finished 14-15 on the season, which was our first losing season in 34 years. This was also the day the drumbeats got too loud to ignore, and it became impossible, as an IU fan, to support Mike Davis.

On March 13, 2005, Davis's team lost to Vanderbilt in the first round of the NIT. On February 16, 2006, Davis announced his resignation effective at the end of the season. A shout of joy was heard from the rafters and parapets. The coaching search for one of the most storied programs in basketball began. The first coaching search at Indiana since Bob Knight was hired in 1971.

On March 29, 2006, Ted Kitchell and Kent Benson got really, really pissed off, and although it was difficult to get them to take a public stand, eventually Kitchell tipped his hand ever so slightly when he said, "I wouldn't hire [Kelvin Sampson] to coach my fifth grade girl's team." Then Indiana University President, Adam Herbert, agreed with Kitchell, choosing not to hire Sampson to coach his fifth grade girl's team, but rather to coach the Indiana Men's Basketball Team, despite Sampson being under NCAA sanctions for 577 impermissible phone calls made to recruits over five years while he was at Oklahoma. Welcome to "Itchy & Scratchy Land," where absolutely nothing can possib-lye go wrong.

On May 25, 2006, the NCAA announced the sanctions for Sampson's "deliberate non-compliance" while he was at Oklahoma, including restrictions on phone calls and off campus recruiting. Those sanctions transferred to Indiana with him.

164

In May 2007, when the restrictions were lifted, Sampson went into Athletic Director, Rick Greenspan's office where they celebrated with high-fives. Take a minute to put that picture in your head. Then consider that Sampson was really throwing those high-fives because he thought he got away with bending and breaking the rules for the past year.

Try not to throw something.

In July 2007, IU conducted an annual compliance review for all sports and initially discovered three-way calls contrary to the committee's penalties.

On October 3, IU filed a report with the NCAA detailing over 100 impermissible phone calls made by Sampson and his coaching staff during the year they were on probation. Focus on that for a second. At Oklahoma, Sampson made 577 impermissible phone calls over five years, which breaks down to just over 100 impermissible calls per year, making the year that he was on probation 100 percent consistent with every other year he spent as a head coach this century. There's something to be said about consistency.[71]

IU forfeited one scholarship for the upcoming year, extended the recruiting restrictions on Sampson, and didn't give him his $500,000 raise. Over the next five months, the NCAA and the university looked into the self-reported violations.

On February 8, 2008, the NCAA sent their findings to the school, which brings us to where we started. Kelvin Sampson is a cheater and a liar. He and his staff, former assistant coaches Rob Senderoff and Jeff Meyer made over 100 impermissible phone calls to recruits.

---

[71] See Chapter 2

Wait a minute, I hear you saying, we already knew that. We learned about that in October when they fired Senderoff and we were appeased. Remember our appeasement? What's the big deal?

The big deal is this part. "It is alleged that (A) during the period of time beginning May 25, 2006, through May 24, 2007, Kelvin Sampson, head men's basketball coach, acted contrary to the NCAA principles of ethical conduct when he knowingly violated recruiting restrictions imposed by the NCAA legislation; (B) Sampson failed to deport himself in accordance with the generally recognized high standard of honesty normally associated with the conduct and administration of intercollegiate athletics by providing the institution and the NCAA enforcement staff false or misleading information; and (C) Sampson failed to promote an atmosphere of compliance within the men's basketball program and failed to monitor the activities regarding compliance of one or more of his assistant coaches."

In October, it was IU telling the NCAA that they thought they found some problems. This was the NCAA saying, you're damn skippy you found some problems and while we were investigating it, Sampson lied to us.

In other words, he broke the rules. He knew he broke the rules. And when we asked him about it, he lied to us.

What do Faye Dunaway, Greg Evigan, Patrick McGoohan, Bill Shatner, and George Hamilton all have in common? They all know what it's like to be doggedly pursued by an investigator who knows they committed a crime and won't let up until he proves it. They were all interviewed, left to stew, interviewed again, left once again to try and work their way out of the trap they were caught up in, and then re-interviewed just before Detective Columbo proved their guilt.

That feeling of thinking that you've gotten away with something, only to have someone come back repeatedly to chip away at your story until it becomes clear that he knows what you did, and what's worse, won't let it go and let you go on about your life, must be brutal. You know who you could ask? Kelvin Sampson.

On October 3, Indiana University filed a report with the NCAA on the implementation and fulfillment of the penalties that were in place when they identified those three-way calls. They filed reports on October 25 and 26, detailing those three-way calls and identifying them as secondary violations, but not before announcing on October 14 that they had imposed sanctions upon themselves in the standard move intended to lessen the potential penalties from the NCAA.

The NCAA thanked us for the report and lauded IU for flagellating ourselves but wondered if we wouldn't mind too terribly much if they did their own investigation. Enter Detective Columbo.

Never one to rush into, or out of a situation, Columbo waited until November 13 to have his first conversation with the basketball coaching staff, including Jeff Meyer, Ray McCallum, and Kelvin Sampson.

It's worth taking a moment to compare this NCAA investigation to the others we have studied. There are a number of significant differences. In the 1985 investigation, the NCAA got involved because a newspaper reported years of corruption. In 1988 the NCAA became aware of the rampant corruption at UK because a package en route to a recruit, filled with money, popped open at a shipping facility. In 2007 the NCAA launched an investigation because IU reported they had discovered some problems.

Columbo had gotten quite spry in his old age. It took him nearly three years to complete the same type of investigation at Kentucky (1985 to 1988). It took them just over a year to complete their investigation following Dwane Casey's ill-fated and ill-conceived plan to mail $1,000 to Chris Mills in early 1988. And in 2007, the good detective spent only spent two and half months in the same rumpled trench coat interviewing members of the athletic staff as well as parents of the recruits who were involved in these phone calls.

The responses of the universities were very different as well. In 1985 UK provided little to no help to the NCAA in their investigation. Their position was to deny, deny, deny and if that didn't work, get in the way. In 1988, UK President David Roselle took a different tactic by cooperating with the NCAA in hopes of garnering some sympathy and lessening the penalties. In 2007, IU followed the 1988 UK approach by being openly cooperative, but went even further than 1988 UK.

Kentucky spent considerable time and money fighting in court to keep the documentation of their investigation and their response to the NCAA from becoming public record. At every turn they fought the publication of these documents. Indiana University released their response to the NCAA, and the case summary with some names crossed out. You can read everything you would want to read about this investigation.[72] This is not true of any of the Kentucky investigations.

The one thing they all have in common is that the NCAA had absolutely no role in uncovering these violations initially. The NCAA is great at looking into things they already know about, but ferreting out cheating on their own is not what they do.

On January 29, in between the UConn game and our trip to

---

[72] Clearly, I did

Wisconsin, Columbo walked up to Kelvin Sampson and said, "Oh, one more thing." He conducted a follow-up interview that should have signaled to Sampson that the jig was very nearly up.

When Columbo went back and looked at the transcripts of all of his conversations with Sampson, it must have made his head spin. Sampson was asked a number of times in both interviews about caller ID and whether he looked at it when recruits called. Sampson said all of the following:

"Sometimes I saw the numbers"

"It didn't matter, I would answer the phone."

"The caller ID at home showed up after the second ring"

"There was no caller ID at home."

"I may glance at it [the caller ID] but as I was going from the couch to the front door, I'm just trying to get reception."

"No, I don't always look at the caller ID. If it's a number I didn't recognize, I'm trying to search to see who it is ..."

"I tried to stay away. The Morris twins' AAU coach, I tried to stay away from his calls cause he called me constantly."

"These kids today have so many different cell phone numbers."

In response to questions about his participation in three-way phone calls subsequent to clarification from the NCAA that those kinds of calls were right out, Sampson said the following:

"I wasn't aware I was receiving three-way calls"

"Yeah, he [Senderoff] said that these kids would call … and he patched 'em in cause they were on the phone to me to begin with. And he was acting as an operator."

"So, you [Kelvin Sampson] had no knowledge that Senderoff was connecting you to a prospect or connecting you to a prospect via a three-way call?"

"Both. My first knowledge of the three-way call was in July"

"I think it was sometime in June when we received the … clarification memo and in there was about the three-way."

But my all time favorite Sampson three-way call/caller ID response is the following:

"Rob Senderoff called me a lot as did all my other assistant coaches. When that cell phone rang, uh, regardless of when it was, I would answer. If, if I had even looked at Rob's number and said this is Rob, uh, Senderoff calling, and I said hello and it was a prospect calling, it would not have registered with me one minute that this was Rob Senderoff calling me with a prospect and I'm involved in a three-way call. At no point would I have thought that cuz I knew that I could not accept a three-way call. If I had thought that was a three-way call, I would have hung up and reported it."

Let's parse that response for a moment, because it's far too brilliant to just read once and move on. In that one paragraph he gives every possible answer to the question.

Answer 1: "When that phone rang, regardless of when it was, I would answer." Or, I didn't even bother to look at the caller ID.

Answer 2: "If, if I had even looked at Rob's number and said this Rob, uh, Senderoff calling, and I said hello and it was a prospect calling, it would not have registered with me one minute that this was Rob Senderfoff calling me with a prospect and I'm involved in a three-way call." Or, even when I did look at the caller ID, which I just said I never did, I wouldn't have put it together that the person on the other end wasn't the same person who showed up on caller ID.

Answer 3: "At no point would I have thought that 'cuz I knew I could not accept a three-way call." Or, even though I don't look at caller ID, when I did look at the caller ID and registered that the person on the phone wasn't the same as the person who called me, which it wouldn't because like I said, that wouldn't have registered with me, it couldn't have been a three-way call, cuz those are wrong and I don't do wrong things.

Answer 4: "If I had thought that was a three-way call, I would have hung up and reported it." Or, I never look at caller ID, but when I look at caller ID I never would have thought it was a three-way call cuz those are wrong and if it had been a three-way call I would have called and told you about it right away, so the fact that I didn't immediately report them means they weren't three-way calls, see?

Aside from saying he's a cheater and a liar the NCAA said that this didn't constitute secondary violations, like the university claimed. This constituted five major violations. A hearing was set for June to address these findings, but waiting until June was not an option.

And thus began the countdown. Unlike October, when the reaction toward Sampson was split, but leaned toward a wait and see point-of-view. We waited. We saw. We were done. This was a gots to go situation. And it was a gots to go NOW situation.

Had the option been given to hide-strap his ass to a pine rail and send him up the Monon Line, George would have had to fight me for his place at the front of the line.

The Gary Condit Award for person whose story got completely buried by a much larger story is AJ Ratliff. On February 12, IU released a statement on Ratliff's decision to leave the team by Samspon saying only "Both of us agreed that it was in his best interest to focus on himself and work through his personal issues. We wish him the best."

Ratliff had missed the previous two games to deal with those same "personal issues." It was a strange end to a bumpy season for Ratliff, who started the year off academically ineligible to play, and then regained his eligibility only to suffer an ankle injury that further delayed his return. He only played in nine games and was never the contributor that I, and many others, thought he would be.

But only a few hours after that announcement was made the Associated Press ran the story that the NCAA allegations had been sent to IU and that they would be made public on February 13.

From a basketball perspective, the timing of this couldn't have been worse. There was now a Scott the Engineer-sized black cloud hanging over the program as the public digested the allegations. Sampson was left in place to coach the Wisconsin game that Wednesday night.

This was a huge match-up. We were ranked 12th (9-1 in conference), Wisconsin was ranked 14th (9-2 in conference) and with home games coming up against Michigan State and Purdue, three wins would almost seal up a share of the title for us.

But, as important as the game was to the season, and as much as I wanted and expected a Big Ten title and Final Four run from this team, I was trapped in a glass house of emotion, with very little time to figure out how I could continue to support this team if what the NCAA was saying was true about its leadership. How could I be like all those UK fans who called for President Roselle's ouster and blamed him for helping the NCAA while claiming that Cliff Hagan and Eddie Sutton should remain? Would supporting this team help contribute to an atmosphere of cheating that would infect it for decades to come? It was a moral dilemma and one that was not easily solved.

What do you do when two things you've believed in strongly your entire life come into direct conflict? For example, what if you grew up idolizing Michael Jackson as your favorite musician, but also believing that pedophilia was bad? Or, maybe the best example of all, what if, in late 1988 you were a true Hulkamaniac but also suffered from Macho Madness?

The late 1980s were a much different time in the world of professional wrestling. Long before the days of Monday Night Raw and Pay Per View events every month story lines took a lot longer to develop. Instead of a disagreement growing to real heat in about three weeks, heat built over longer periods of time.

When 1987 began, there was only one Pay Per View event in the WWF, *Wrestlemania*. It was the year that wrestling hit new heights.

The last weekend in March 1987 was an unforgettable weekend. It was the weekend we captured the NCAA title in New Orleans but it was so much more than that. I was staying with my cousins because my parents made the trip to New Orleans for the Final Four. Excited beyond words from our victory the day before (and waiting for what would be the greatest moment of my childhood on Monday, March 30) we set our 11 year-old minds to the prospect of *Wrestlemania III*. Armed with the knowledge of the start time for the event and the fact that it was on Pay Per View, Brian and I sat down in front of the TV.

What we were not armed with, however, was a complete understanding of what "Pay Per View" meant. Here was my logic: We paid for cable, but my attempts to watch *Wrestlemania II* the year before by flipping through every channel on our set-top cable box had been unsuccessful. So it wasn't on regular cable. My cousins got Showtime, a statement that was not true of my parents. I knew you had to pay to view these channels, so I thought there was a decent chance *Wrestlemania* would be on Showtime. It was not.

Why, you may ask, did you not merely ask if you could order the Pay Per View once you figured out it wasn't on Showtime? For those of you who have not my Aunt Carol, let me tell you a story that may illuminate for you why the thought of asking her to order this would never have entered my mind. For those of you who have, no story is necessary, but you can read it anyway.

During this or some other visit to their house, we sat down to eat dinner. Carol had a rule that you could choose two items on the table not to eat, but you had to eat at least a little bit of everything else. God help my poor little brother, all of seven or eight years-old, who was a picky eater and did not like three of the items on the table. He informed my aunt that he would not be eating the cottage cheese (item three on his list of won'ts). The discussion went like this.

Michael: "I won't eat that gross cottage cheese."

174

Carol: "Yes you will."

Michael: "I won't!"

Carol: "You damn well will, you little shit!"[73]

Michael: "If I eat that I'll puke!" *Tears beginning to stream down his face*

Carol: "If you puke, I'll make you eat the puke."

Suddenly very scared and completely convinced that she would make him eat his own puke, Michael ate the cottage cheese. Now, I was older and a much more sophisticated man of the world at 11 and I knew she wasn't really going to make him eat his own puke. But, I didn't know *for sure*. And the idea of asking a woman who may or may not make children eat their own puke if she would spend $40 for you to watch wrestling didn't seem like the wisest move.

So, I didn't see what unfolded that day for quite a while, but it was the moment that wrestling went big time. In front of 93,173 fans in the Pontiac Silverdome, Hulk Hogan squared off against the Eighth Wonder of the World, Andre The Giant.

Andre had been an ally of Hogan's until, during an episode of Piper's Pit, Bobby "The Brain" Heenan presented himself as The Giant's manager and a clearly pissed off Giant challenged Hogan to a title match at *Wrestlemania III*. He grabbed Hogan's shirt and tore it and his gold cross necklace from the Champ's neck. This heel turn by The Giant set up one of the most anticipated match ups of all time.

---

[73] I'm paraphrasing here, but "little shit" was possibly her favorite two word combination, so while I'll not vouch that she said it here, it's as safe as assuming Hulk Hogan used the word "Brother" in a sentence.

Early in the main event, Hogan attempted to lift the 500+-pound Giant off the ground to body slam him. He couldn't and Andre fell on top of Hogan. The count was stopped at two as Hogan got his shoulder off the mat, but this close call would be the cause of much controversy after the match, which went on for some time before Hogan attempted to slam The Giant again. This time, he summoned the strength of all the Hulkamaniacs in attendance, those watching on Pay Per View and those, like me, not watching, but rooting for the Hulkster, and lifted The Giant off the ground, slammed him to the mat and hit him with the leg drop. He covered Andre for the win, igniting a fire that refused to die out.

While Hogan was still flying high off the defeat of Andre at *Wrestlemania III*, former Intercontinental Champion Randy "Macho Man" Savage was waging his own battle with The Honky Tonk Man. In September 1987, during a title match, the Hart Foundation insinuated themselves into the match to aid Honky Tonk and while they were triple-teaming Savage and preparing to break a guitar over his head, Savage's manager, the lovely Miss Elizabeth, tried to intervene, only to have the Honky Tonk Man shove her to the ground. She ran backstage, seemingly deserting her man. She returned moments later with Hulk Hogan, who ran to Savage's rescue and an uneasy partnership was formed.

Knowing they had a goldmine on their hands, the WWF decided to add more Pay Per View events, the first being the *Survivor Series* on Thanksgiving night 1987.

The main event of *Survivor Series* was between a team lead by Hogan and a team lead by Andre The Giant. This time The Giant was the last man standing, but Hogan couldn't stand that and attacked him with a chair after the match, clearing the ring for the pose down that everyone wanted to see.

This set the stage for one more title rematch between the two, on live television, in February 1988 from Indianapolis. By this time The Giant had come under the sway of the Million Dollar Man, Ted Dibiase. Dibiase hired some sort of Dave Hepner lookalike to ref the match, who had his back turned when Hogan pinned The Giant for a five count, but managed to be right on top of it when The Giant pinned Hogan. Hulk's shoulder was up prior to the two count this time, but the fake Dave Hepner didn't see it and awarded the match and the title to The Giant, who then surrendered the belt to Dibiase. Andre the Giant and the fake Dave Hoepner had a price.

When he surrendered the title to Dibiase, commissioner Jack Tunney had to step in and make a ruling on the legality of such an action. It was ruled illegal and the title was vacated. To fill the vacant title a tournament was set up for *Wrestlemania IV*, with the winner being crowned the undisputed WWF Heavy Weight Champion.

Here's the problem when you have one bankable superstar; eventually people get tired of him, or he wants to take a vacation. Hulk Hogan had been, prior to his questionable defeat in Indianapolis, the WWF champion for over four years. *Wrestlemania III* had upped the stakes for the WWF, and a main event rematch between Hulk Hogan and Andre the Giant would be a letdown, so the selection committee decided to give Hogan and Andre the Giant first round byes, setting them up to fight each other early in the tournament. And in what has to be the least consistently enforced rule in all of sports[74] the match ended in a double count out, disqualifying both men and leaving a clear path for Ted Dibiase to make it to the title match.

His opponent was none other than the Macho Man, who faced

[74] Shut up, alright. I know it's not real.

incredible odds. Virgil, the Million Dollar Man's bodyguard (a concept I could not wrap my head around at age 12. Why would a man who fights people for a living need a bodyguard at work? This, of course was years before Mike Tyson needed a bodyguard to keep him from eating the children that his opponents didn't have) was not at ring side, so that position was taken by Andre the Giant.

The battle of ringside companions raged heavily throughout the match, in that Gorilla Monsoon and Jesse "the Body" Ventura couldn't shut up about the fact that Miss Elizabeth versus Andre the Giant would not be a fair fight.

Fair? No. Awesome? Hell yes!

Finally seeing she was outmatched, and knowing that there was more to life than being really, really, really ridiculously good-looking, Miss Elizabeth went backstage. She returned a moment later with, oh hell, you know who she brought back.

While the referee was busy chastising Andre the Giant for interfering in the match, Hulk Hogan bravely climbed into the ring and heroically whacked DiBiase on the back of the head with a steel chair. Macho, dazed and unsure about what just happened, climbed the ropes, landed his patented flying elbow,[75] and pinned DiBiase for the title.

This act of bravery on Hogan's part helped secure the title for Savage and officially formed the Mega Powers! Having formed the most powerful partnership since Bill Cosby and new Coke, Hogan promptly took six months off.

---

[75] A search of Google patents uncovered no such patent on file in the United States.

Savage continued to feud with DiBiase over the next few months before challenging Dibiase and The Giant to a tag-team battle at *SummerSlam*, the next addition to the Pay Per View catalogue, with a mystery partner of his choosing. He chose, oh hell, I can't fool you, you know who it was.

The Mega Powers were the embodiment of Indiana basketball. Randy Savage was all about winning at any cost. He had held multiple lesser titles in his career and had become a fan favorite. Hulk Hogan was the anthropomorphification of doing things the right way. He was as famous for winning as he was for why he won; the three pillars of training, prayers, and vitamins. It wasn't until these two wrestling forces combined that Savage was able to win the heavyweight title. Showing what all Hoosiers know, you cannot have winning without doing things the right way.

The glory could not last for the Mega Powers, and the source of their friction was one person, Miss Elizabeth. "Winning" was getting jealous of Elizabeth's relationship with "doing the right thing" and accused "doing the right thing" of having "jealous eyes." Elizabeth couldn't make a choice between the two leading to the inevitable collision at *Wrestlemania V*.[76]

And that's when we had to decide whose side we were on. Were we Hulkamaniacs, concerned with doing things the right way, or were we with the Macho Man and all about winning at any cost?

As you can see, I've been tested. We've all been tested. And when it comes to moral quandaries, there is little better preparation for a true examination of one's personal beliefs than watching the Mega Powers

---

[76] That's right, this has been going on for two years now.

collide. In 1989, I made the right choice. I was a Hulkamaniac and rejoiced when he dropped the leg on Savage to regain his title, but it wasn't an easy choice, and Hoosier fans faced the same choice nearly 20 years later.

From this point forward there were four choices: 1.) Wait and see what happened. This was the coward's way out. As Miss Elizabeth found out, you can't wait until the match is over and then hope everything works out alright. Walk right side of road, safe. Walk left side of road, safe. Walk middle, sooner or later, squish. Just like grape; 2.) Support Sampson and the team, claim that these infractions were no big deal, and take my first step toward the Dark Side, in other words, be a Kentucky fan; 3.) Condemn both Sampson and the team. Cheer for the double count out, where both sides lose; or 4.) Take a very nuanced position that condemns Sampson but manages to still support the fruit of his poisonous tree, which is, at best, a slightly smaller step toward the Dark Side.

None of these were great options, because unlike *Wrestlemania V*, at the end of this bout, there wasn't going to be a clean solution. But prior to the Wisconsin game, Fish and Leary laid the argument for position four, and as much as it shocked me, I agreed with Leary.

"There's not a whole lot that we can do and it's not going to affect the administration's point-of-view or perspective on what they're going to do, so really all you can do as an Indiana fan right now is support the basketball team," said Leary, "and that's the real key. These kids deserve it. DJ White deserves it especially. He's stayed here for four years, put his time into Indiana University and hung with this school, and a lot of people thought he could have gone pro last year and the year before and he stuck out his four years and he deserves everyone to support him."

What had DJ ever done but stick with IU through some of the

180

toughest times, grown as a player, and shown himself to be nothing but a great player and person? To not support him, and the other players, who to no one's knowledge at this point, had done anything wrong seemed inexcusable.

A balance had been struck, providing me with some narrow safe ground where I could continue to root for this team while being completely disgusted with the actions of Kelvin Sampson. Squish? Just like grape?

Prior to the game, Greenspan held a press conference where he gave a very brief description of what the university would do moving forward and expressed disappointment that there were any allegations of impropriety. Associate Director of Athletics, Grace Calhoun, said, "Our response to these allegations is due in 90 days, which is on or around May 8, and we do plan to release a report shortly thereafter. IU will appear before the Committee on Infractions on June 14, and the charges should be adjudicated within 30 days or so of that hearing."

Any delay on the part of the university, even waiting for the 90 day period to pass, before taking decisive action was going to be a huge mistake, but by the tip-off this was all we had from the university as far as a plan went. All of that would change in the morning, but first there was a game to play.

And they played. This was a game, much like the Illinois game, where this team managed to put all of the things out of their minds that didn't matter and play basketball. They played with anger in this game. I think the anger was misdirected, but I'm not sure you can win if you are pissed at your coach for being a giant turd. You have to view it as the rest of the world is out to get us, so let's bunch together in one of those *300* style phalanx formations, leaving no gaps, and attack.

It was a back and forth battle for most of the game. Wisconsin reserve guard, Jason Bohanon, torched us from the perimeter with six three-pointers. DJ had 17 points and eight rebounds and EJ had another very good offensive game, scoring 23 points, 9-10 from the free throw line, including two with 12.5 seconds to go to give us a 66-65 lead. But it wasn't enough, as Brian Butch banked in a three-pointer with four seconds to play to give Wisconsin the 68-66 win and an edge in the Big Ten standings. If it ever came to a tie breaker, they had beat us twice.

It turns out that snotty reporter was right when he asked Sampson whether our schedule in December was too soft. While Wisconsin was traveling to Austin to play Texas in their home gym, we were busy padding our record with Coppin State, Chicago State, and Western Carolina.

It was the perfect ending to the perfect day.

Interlude Ten: Friends, Hoosiers, Countrymen

During the post game press conference Kelvin Sampson had this to say about that:

"I have a statement that I would like to read. Then I'm not going to comment, not going to comment, nor can I comment anymore on it. I'm aware that the NCAA has issued a Notice of Allegations. The allegations that I knowingly acted contrary to the sanctions imposed on me for violations that occurred while I was at Oklahoma are not true. I have never *intentionally* [Sampson's emphasis] provided false or misleading information to the NCAA. I intend to work within the NCAA process on this matter and I look forward to my opportunity to do so. I do not anticipate having any further comment until after the process has been concluded and I have had a chance to address the allegations with the Committee on Infractions."

The noble Sampson

Hath told you there are allegations;

If it is so, is it a grievous situation;

And grievously will Sampson answer them;

Here under leave of the NCAA and the rest—

For Sampson is an honourable man;

So are his actions, they are all honourable;

Come I to speak at this press conference,

These allegations seem just to me:

But Sampson says they are false;

And Sampson is an honourable man.

The NCAA have done months of investigation

Interviewed many witnesses

Could their conclusions be in err?

When they asked him did he do it, he said no

All other witnesses said yes

Yet Sampson says he never intentionally mislead

And Sampson is an honourable man

You all had chance to read the allegations

They mention thrice-way calling

Which he did thrice refuse knowledge of

Was this misleading?

Yet Sampson says he did not mislead

And, sure, he is an honourable man.

I speak not to disprove what Sampson spoke,

But I am here to speak what I do know

You all love this program, not without cause

What cause withholds you then, to mourn for it?

"I'm sorry Bob. You guys all do a great job. I mean you do. And I know you have a job to do, but I can't, I just can't talk about this. I mean, I hope you understand my situation."

I understand his situation.

He says he cannot speak of it

And he is an honourable man

Chapter Eleven: Things We Said Today

It's time to take the training wheels off. You are going to be given a chance to practice your Packer Method skills right now. The coverage following the Wisconsin game spread far beyond the normal bounds of the Indianapolis Star, the Louisville Courier-Journal, the Fort Wayne News-Sentinel, the Fort Wayne Journal Gazette, the Bloomington Herald-Times, other Indiana newspapers, and the intermittent coverage by the Chicago Tribune. There were also numerous articles and columns on CBS.com, ESPN.com, and every other sport-related.com you can come up with.

Your very short assignment is to create the percentage of these pieces that were about the actual game. If you would like to ease into the Packer Method, you can create the percentage of the pieces that think IU should back Kelvin Sampson and show their support by offering him a contract extension. You should have fabricated your percentages by now. It's cheating to do it once you have actual information on which to base your opinion.

Ben Smith of the Journal Gazette suggested the Sampson resign immediately to avoid hurting the program even more, as Mike Davis did two years ago. This position ignores one critical piece of information, which is that Sampson's actions to date had not shown a desire to avoid hurting the program. It's like asking a puppy-stabber to write a check to the ASPCA.

Skip Myslenski of the Chicago Tribune did not proffer an opinion, but rather pointed out the numerous areas in Sampson's contract that seemed to make it possible for IU to fire him. As Chris Rock said, "I'm not saying I would have killed the bitch, but I understand."

Reggie Hayes of the Fort Wayne News-Sentinel echoed a sentiment found in Ben Smith's crosstown piece and in the hearts of many IU fans. There's enough blame gravy left on the plate for all of us to pick up Rick Greenspan like a piece of bread and sop up the excess.

Pat Forde of ESPN.com took quite the stand when he stated, in no uncertain terms, that "IU's best course of action might be to suspend Sampson immediately." Forde could have found his stones in Gregg Doyel's pocket. Over on CBS.com Doyel threw a high hard one. "Indiana has no choice, it must fire Sampson—now." No room for interpretation there. Good on ya, Gregg.

Doyel's colleague at CBS.com, Miss Gary Parish, and I say 'Miss' because he seems to have missed the point all together, thought that Sampson was now coaching for his "Indiana career." To quote Myra Fleener, "I think it goes a little bit deeper than one game. Don't you?"

Mike DeCourcy, of the *SportingNews*, suggested a post-season coaching ban on Sampson. Sorry, Mike, but this doesn't go nearly far enough. He was suggesting that Sampson be allowed to roam the sidelines, in limbo, for seven more games and then have to sit for tournament play. Every game he is allowed to coach this team is a big "eff you" to the NCAA which would have completely undone whatever goodwill we engendered by sanctioning ourselves in October.

Dear NCAA,

This notice of five major violations is a pretty big deal. We think it's big, too. Tell you what, how about we wait another month and then we'll punish him. You see, we've got these games to play first. They're pretty important. Kthnxbye.

And finally, Mark Schlabach, of ESPN.com was the first to mention something that I'm sure was bound to come up eventually. "Oddly enough, Knight might be looking for work." It was too soon for predictions about the next coach when we still had one, however temporarily, and at least a month of basketball to go, but there was no way Bob Knight would become the once and future coach of Indiana basketball. Both Knight and I could have seen that in his drinking glass crystal ball. The very idea is laughable. Let's focus on one thing at a time, maybe two. Getting rid of Kelvin Sampson, and beating Michigan State on Saturday, hopefully in that order.

That was how the media responded Valentine's Day morning. Can you feel the love? President McRobbie was a little slower to pull the trigger, but his aim was far more accurate. On Friday afternoon, February 15, McRobbie called a press conference to announce what the university's response would be. He said the following:

Today I am announcing that I've directed the athletics director to oversee an immediate investigation of these new allegations and make an assessment as to whether they are credible and accurate. I've given him seven days as of now to complete this task. I am deeply disappointed by these allegations, and I share that disappointment with all those who love and support Indiana University. I fully understand the desire by many people for us to move quickly to bring this situation to resolution, and we intend to do just that. When this investigation is completed, the athletics director will use the findings to guide him in making a recommendation to me as to what our next step will be. I want to make clear that all of us are going into this with no presumptions. I do not know what conclusions the investigators will come to regarding these new allegations. Let there be no doubt, these are serious allegations of misconduct. As president, I believe the most important measure of our success in intercollegiate athletics is not in the win-loss column. It is in how we measure up to our own high standards of good sportsmanship, academic success, the welfare of our student athletes and playing by the rules.

That's what President McRobbie said, but here's what he meant. The NCAA took four months to complete their investigation. We took two days to read their findings. We're announcing a seven-day investigation for two reasons: 1.) We're a little worried that if we just fire him right now he'll be able to sue us for breach of contract so we're giving him due process, and while that's complete bullshit, we've got to cover our asses here, and 2.) We need a little time to work out the details, because as much as this seems like enough cause to fire him, we're probably going to have to do some sort of buyout, and that takes lawyers and time.

Have you ever spent the night at a friend's house, or had one spend the night at yours, on the same night the parents, be they yours or theirs, got into a huge screaming match?

For the Michigan State game we were the ESPN Saturday night game of the week. As part of that honor, the Game Day crew came to town. They did their show from Bloomington all day. It's usually a lot of fun and a great way to showcase the school and the program. You get excited about it the same way you get excited to show your friend your toys and your room. But when your parents fight, or the NCAA has called your coach a lying cheat and the university has started the process that will lead to his mid-season ousting, you'd rather not have company over.

It was pure folly to think that this would all be done with little media scrutiny, but it's one thing to light fireworks off from the crack of your ass, only to have them burn your meat and veg in front of your friends. It's another thing to do that and have your friends post the video on youtube so you can watch it go viral while soaking your boys in a bucket of iced water.

As part of the Game Day crew, Jay Bilas was on-hand for all the pre-game festivities. Bilas is one of the few analysts that is truly a value-add to the game. He brings good insight and is right more often than not. He is also an attorney, so his take on this fiasco was predictable and not wrong. He said that a weeklong investigation probably wasn't long enough. The NCAA gave us 90 days to respond, a date for a hearing and a timeline for when a final determination would be handed down. There's a system in place to deal with things like this and we should allow the system to work.

I'm all for due process, but here's what Jay was missing with this analysis: 1.) If Sampson coached out the end of this season it would look like the university is supporting him and his actions. This could have lead to harsher penalties from the NCAA, 2) The hearing was scheduled for June. That's just the hearing. Their findings wouldn't come down until September at the earliest. If it came back bad, and let's face it, how could it not, we fire Sampson in September and then there would be no time for a proper coaching search, 3.) With this cloud hanging over us, the recruits we had were likely to bolt, maybe not all of them, but enough. How would we replace them in September? Sampson's ability to recruit is over, at least at IU, 4.) What if we made it to the Final Four? I can't imagine the reaction of the IU community if this team were to win with Sampson at the helm. It likely would have all been vacated from the records. You can't really celebrate that kind of accomplishment, can you? UK fans celebrate the '48, '49, '51 and '78 championships, so I guess some can, but I can't, and 5.) We needed to move on. The longer we waited to start the next phase of IU basketball, the harder it was going to be to fix this mess.

Leave it Dick Vitale to cut right to heart of the matter, as he did during his call of the game. "I have a better chance of beating Matt Damon and Brad Pitt for sexiest man in all of television than [Kelvin Sampson] does of surviving." But he went further. "When you have that recommendation that is going to be handed down by Athletic Director, Rick Greenspan, he better make sure he recommends, at the same time, that the athletic director be let go as well, when he makes that recommendation because he needs to be accountable. He hired Mr. Sampson, knowing about all those calls and knowing that he was on penalties and sanctions at Oklahoma, so he has to be accountable and responsible as the leader of Indiana athletics"

The players, when they spoke about it, predictably rallied around their coach. EJ said, "I came to Indiana to not only go to the postseason, but to be coached by Kelvin Sampson in the postseason. For them to take that away from us makes this season seem worthless." And that's the ballgame boys and girls. When the players start talking about "them taking that away from us" and the season being worthless you might as well pack it in, cuz it's over.

When Sampson was introduced prior to the game there were no boos or cheers. There was nothing. The crowd seemed to be unsure of how to react. They wanted to support the team and they wanted a win, so booing Sampson would have been acting against those interests, especially with the team closing ranks around Sampson, but I don't see how he could have been cheered.

Vitale did not let up during the game. Not only did he mention Bob Knight less than two minutes into the game (if you took the under on that, you won), he once again voiced his belief that the court should be named after Knight. At the 17:18 mark in the first half Dick Vitale got it right and earned lifetime love from every IU fan. Sampson had told the players, "In life, sometimes things don't work out the way you want. They're not fair. You can't control the situation. You (the players) can't control, you can't affect the outcome of what's going on here. You just worry about playing basketball and I promise you that when I'm with you I'll think of nothing else but coaching you."

To which Vitale replied, "I'll tell you this very simply, you can control the actions of you and your staff in handling the rules and regulations you must abide to. I mean 577 calls! I can buy two, or three, or four, or five, but let's get real here. And then you come to Indiana and you get into the same scenario."

Vitale wasn't done. Rick Greenspan told Erin Andrews "It would be faulty to assume that the decision into hiring a head coach is singularly made by an athletic director."

Vitale. Aim. Fire. "I don't like to hear when other people who were involved in making the decision, because, to me, that's simply saying 'the heat is on, baby and it's time for me to move away from the heat and I don't want to be blamed for that decision.' I say that's a no-no. And that's not leadership. That's not a man that's running the program who's taking charge. He hired Kelvin Sampson. Make no bones about it. He stood there and knew about the allegations."

192

That night, I heard all my rage coming out of Dick Vitale's mouth.

Vitale came out strongly against Eddie Sutton in 1989 as well, and he was skewered for it by UK fans. I'm shocked UK fans and I had a different reaction to Vitale calling out our coach and AD when they had done something wrong.

The game itself, clearly secondary to everything else that was going on, was a very close one in the first half. Until, that is, the 5:01 mark, when DJ went down with a knee injury. From that point to the end of the half we pulled away from Michigan State to lead by eight at the half.

DJ never returned and the game never got closer. We won this game by 19 points, which, again is not the story, but before the game ended something happened that made me ashamed to be an IU fan.

At the 1:48 mark in the second half with the game well in hand, thanks to the hard work of the team, the crowd broke into the Kel-Vin Samp-Son cheer. Is this who we are? Are IU fans really willing to sell out what we've always said we believed in because we won a basketball game? Are we Kentucky fans, supporting Eddie Sutton while his coaches paid recruits and his recruits cheated on the ACT?

I can't say with any certainty how I would have reacted had I been in Assembly Hall that night. The emotions of a crowd can sweep people away, but I'd be shocked if I took part in that cheer. If Billy Reed was right in 1988 that the mentality and culture of Kentucky fans was largely to blame for the history of cheating at Kentucky, then what message did cheering for Sampson at the end of that game send about our tolerance for cheating and our willingness to trade what we believe in for victories? Are we not Hulkamaniacs?

After the game, Sampson once again proved that he has very little situational awareness, as he told Don Fischer, "What can you say about the Assembly Hall crowd? Our crowd was unbelievable. It was a great match tonight. Our team played with great passion. Our fans had great passion. It was just a great mix. This was a great night for Hoosier basketball."

We won the game, but there is not a scale on which this night can be weighed as a great one for Hoosier basketball.[77] It was an embarrassment. It was a travesty. It was awful. And it was all Sampson's fault.

Sampson finished the evening with a string of "no comments" and this little gem, "IU basketball is so much bigger than one person."

Our success is bigger than one person. The tradition is bigger than one person. Destroying the whole thing? I think we've seen that can be done by one person.

Sampson got one more chance to not comment on that prior to the Purdue game, which was the last one prior to the terminus of the seven day investigation, when he appear with Don Fischer in *The I'm Contractually Obligated to Suffer Through This Once a Week, But I Can't Believe I Agreed to Do This In Front Of A Bunch Of Students Inside Indiana Basketball Coach's Show.*

I found these shows fascinating all year long. It's not often you get the chance to listen to a sociopath[78] on the radio for an hour every week.

---

[77] Except on the Sampson Syllogism Scale where a win means everything's great!

[78] My own diagnoses. To my knowledge Sampson has never received an official diagnosis from a trained professional explaining exactly what is wrong with him.

It's a golden opportunity to listen and wonder at the machinations of a truly disturbed mind. But this last one set an unreachable bar for uncomfortable. It's the 56-game hit streak of awkward radio.

Fish started out the broadcast by discussing the NBA All-Star game to an undercurrent of sustained, lackluster, applause. This was a game that Sampson clearly did not see. In what has to be the worst scripted back and forth ever heard on radio Sampson said, "Who was the MVP? Lebron James? Well, judging from that reaction, that must have been a really good game."

"One of the better All-Star games," replied Fish.

"I was talkin' about the reaction from these guys. It must have been a really good game against Michigan State." Sampson said while Fish chuckled uncomfortably. Fish had years of experience working Knight through these shows. He had a background of playing the straight man to Knight's sarcasm and question-dodging. And with all that experience producing difficult radio I had never heard him this uncomfortable.

But there was more awkwardness to come before the first commercial break. In discussing the Wisconsin game, Sampson said, "You take away his [Bohanon's] six threes … and you realize how close we were." I can't tell you the number of times I've looked at the guy sitting next to me at a game and said, "Man, you take away the 18 points that one guy scored on us and this would be a nail biter." It's amazing how a big a difference a little thing like 18 points can make in a two-point ball game.

Right before the break, Fish said, "As you said in our pre-game before the ballgame on Saturday, sometimes you live by that three-bank shot and sometimes you die by it. And of course Eric Gordon made one that gave you a chance to go into overtime against Illinois."

To which Sampson replied, "I didn't say that, Fish, you did."

Fish laughed uncomfortably again and said, "We're going to take a commercial break because I've got to collect myself. I feel very awkward."

Don't we all.

Fish felt awkward there because he knew that Sampson said something very much to that effect. What Sampson said, in fact, was "Eerily similar to the long bank shot Eric hit against Illinois. You start banking 'em in from 23 feet, good chance you're gonna win." He said that with no prompting from Fish about the similarities. It was his thought, and for some reason, he decided to lie about it on the radio. Add it to the long list of untruths.

There was one more moment of, at best, tremendous spin and at worst, great self delusion. "If College Game Day shows up, they're honoring your school and the tradition of your school ... If they show up, that means they have respect for your tradition and your program. I can't imagine a better university to go have College Game Day at than Indiana University."

This is true, most of the time. It's also very possible that they go where the story is. They follow the drama. If that drama is caused by a big match up, which is probably why they scheduled IU versus Michigan State in the first place, or whether the drama is caused by the coach being a total lying, cheating douche bag, doesn't matter too much to them. They go where the story is, and the story was in Bloomington that week.

In the land of screened calls, the man with the button is king. Though, how Captain Janks can get through to Larry King to ask questions about Howard Stern's penis and no one can slip one "why are you trying to destroy Indiana basketball?" question past the goalie is quite beyond my capacity.

Anyone who tuned in hoping or expecting to hear Sampson address anything important had never listened to this show before. He didn't take a single question about his cheating, which was not a surprise. And neither was his demeanor. He acted as though nothing out of the ordinary was happening, and that ability to put up such a complete mask was probably what I found so disturbing about him. Baba Booey! Baba Booey!

Purdue games don't get any more important than this one. Depending on the poll you looked at heading into the only meeting between the two teams, IU was ranked 14 and Purdue 15, or vice versa. Purdue was 12-1 in the Big Ten and atop the standings, while IU, courtesy of a ridiculous bank shot by Brian Butch (that was either exactly like, or nothing like, the shot EJ hit at Illinois depending on when you asked Sampson about it), sat at 11-2. With only five games left, this game was set to play a deciding roll in the Big Ten title.

A look ahead at the schedule for IU showed only one real stumbling block, a trip to East Lansing on March 2, while a look ahead for Purdue showed little to be concerned with, save for a trip to Columbus on March 4. A loss here by IU and our Big Ten hopes would likely be dashed, while a win would put us in excellent position to at least tie for the title with the tie breaker in our column.

It was a huge game. It was also the third game in a row where the game was secondary. This was day four of the seven-day investigation and the last game scheduled before the clock was set to run out. This game was a must win, but not with the stakes Sampson would have hoped.

The final question heading into this game was the status of DJ's knee, which kept him out of the entire second half against Michigan State. Sampson said DJ was going to play, but I've heard him give starting lineups with players in it who were suspended so that assurance did little to ease my worried mind.

Sampson had taken to pointing out, following the Wisconsin game, how sometimes stats didn't mean much.[79] After all, we turned the ball over 26 times at Minnesota and won, but turned it over only five times against Wisconsin and lost. See, facts and figures don't mean anything, except when they paint a very clear picture of why you won a game. If I told you that Team A got 43 rebounds while Team B only got 28, Team A shot 48 percent from the field and 88 percent from the line, while Team B shot 35 percent from the field and 52 percent from the line, Team A had one player who had 19 points and 15 rebounds, another player who had 22 while hitting 13-15 from the line, and a third player who had 16 on 4-4 three-point shooting and Team B had players with 17, 12, and 11 who would you say won that game?

What if I told you that Team A scored 77 points and Team B scored 66?

in your face stats haters![80]

The Purdue game capped, without question, the best three-game stretch this team had played all year, and one could be tempted to be really pissed about Butch banking in that three-pointer and costing us a victory in the first of the three. This team played together with passion

---

[79] Like 577, 100, and three-way.

[80] Turnovers were our Marion Barry at the Million Man March. We had 23, in what was otherwise a complete statistical domination.

and a commitment to one another that was inspiring.

One could be tempted to be really pissed at Butch, but if one were to take a step back and big picture this deal, that Butch shot probably wouldn't bother one quite so much because the only stat that mattered any more was three, which was how many days were left before the decision on Sampson's fate would be made.

Interlude Eleven: Who Cares About Phone Calls?

Everyone is entitled to their opinions. And I'm entitled to tell them to shut up. The crowd inside Assembly Hall for the Michigan State and Purdue games proved what I had always thought about IU fans wasn't true, at least not completely. This is dangerous ground for me. If I'm not able to say that all IU fans are one way, how can I say that all Kentucky fans are one way?[81]

These were two big wins at a critical time in the season against two really good teams. And it's always a big deal to beat Purdue. That's what rivalries are all about. But there's a huge leap between cheering for your team, who is playing very good basketball, and making the conscious decision to explicitly cheer for the coach who is in the middle of a seven-day investigation to determine whether he should be fired for cheating and lying.

And enough fans inside Assembly Hall, during both games, decided to chant Sampson's name in unison loud enough for me to hear it clearly through the television. Is this what we believe? Is this who we are? Do we really care about winning more than integrity and honesty? I wonder.

But what made me wonder more than the chanting, which I can understand a little, it's very easy to get wrapped up in the emotion of the win and go along with the energy of the crowd, is a sign I saw that read "who cares about phone calls?"

In Billy Reed's 1988 column in the *Lexington Herald-Leader* entitled, "Big Blue Mentality has Made Time Stand Still" he wrote the following:

---

[81] I don't have an answer for that, except that I can and I will continue to say that all Kentucky fans are one way.

You've heard the party line, maybe even adhered to it. Everybody's against UK. Jealous of the Cats. Wants to bring The Program down. And so on and so forth, ad infinitum. But for dispassionate observers, the obvious conclusion is that nothing much has changed in Lexington over the decades. Coaches, players and fans have come and gone, but the mentality has remained the same. And so long as that mentality exists in Lexington, which may be long after Rex Chapman is in an old folks' home in Owensboro, then UK is going to be susceptible to one embarrassment after another because of the blind, desperate, all-consuming desire to win.

We've all watched what this attitude has fostered in Lexington. I wasn't around when they first broke the rules and had players working for bookies while Adolph Rupp said, hey guys, what's the big deal, it's not like they tried to lose, they just shaved points. But I was around for all but the first few years of Joe B. Hall's reign, when players were routinely being paid by boosters in the locker rooms after the games. And I was around when Dwane Casey mailed cash to the father of a recruit and Eric Manual cheated on the ACT to get into Kentucky.

The reason that every coach at Kentucky from 1930 to 1990 ran a dirty program is because the fans allowed it. They supported it. They excused the rule breaking with logic, like everyone else is doing it, and we're being set up.

And they cheered. Loudly. They idolized Adolph Rupp. And Joe B. Hall, who instead of being a pariah for running a program where his players had sugar daddies like Maynard Hogg, who would give players money whenever they needed it, is still a visible part of the Kentucky basketball landscape, hosting a radio show with former U of L coach Denny Crum. They cared only about winning.

And the fact that after two wins our fans were willing to ignore all the things we've ever said about ourselves, about how it's important to do things the right way, to chant Kel-vin Samp-son and that at least one ass-basket (not the one on the cover. That's a recreation) took out a poster board and marker and took the time to write, in letters big enough to be broadcast across the country "who cares about phone calls?"

The answer is I do. The NCAA seems to. You should, too. And as we found out three days later, so did the university.

Chapter Twelve: Of Course Because You Are a Character Does Not Mean You Have Character

"From Bloomington, IN," the flash apparently official, "Kelvin Sampson has resigned as Head Men's Basketball Coach for Indiana University."

Athletic Director, Rick Greenspan, announced at a press conference on February 22, that the university accepted "the immediate resignation" of Coach Kelvin Sampson. Sampson released a statement to the press saying:

I have made the very difficult decision to leave my position as head coach of the men's basketball team at Indiana University. While I'm saddened that I will not have the opportunity to continue to coach these student athletes, I feel that it is in the best interest of the program for me to step aside at this time. I wish my players and staff nothing but the best for the remainder of the season. They are all truly incredible people. As I have previously stated, I welcome the opportunity to go before the Committee on Infractions in June. I look forward to getting back on the basketball court in the very near future.

As part of his resignation, Sampson accepted a $750,000 buyout and agreed not to sue the university for wrongful termination. Dan Dakich was named the Interim Head Coach for the remainder of the season and Ray McCallum was named assistant to the regional manager.

Now, I'm no fancy big city lawyer, but I have a hard time believing that when you are hired away from a school that is in the process of being penalized for your transgressions, I don't know, say, making 577 impermissible phone calls, the contract you sign at the new school doesn't have language in it to the effect of: *If you (the douche signing the contract) do the exact same illegal crap you were doing at your previous job that led to the NCAA imposing sanctions upon both you and the school at which you used to work now that you are working for us, we (the complete ass-baskets that decided to hire you in the first place) have the right to fire your ass and not pay you any kind of buy out because you're a big cheater or are simply too stupid to live. May God Have Mercy on your soul.*

Again, not being a fancy big city lawyer, here's what his contract did say that would seem to support my notion that we could have told him not to let the door hit him on the ass on the way out.

Article II, Section 2.01, Subsection B states, "The Employee further agrees to abide by and comply with the constitution, bylaws and interpretations of the NCAA and all NCAA, Big Ten Conference, and University rules and regulations relating to the conduct and administration of the men's basketball program, including but not limited to, recruiting rules. In the event that the Employee becomes aware, or has reasonable cause to believe, that violations of such constitution, bylaws, interpretations, rules or regulations may have taken place, he shall report the same in writing promptly to the Director of Athletics ("Director of Athletics") and the Faculty Athletics Representative of the University."

204

Subsection C of the same Article and Section said "This position has these additional specific responsibilities:

Maintain an environment where the pursuit of higher education is a priority as reflected by class attendance, grade point averages, and graduation rates;

Oversee recruiting evaluations, official visits, and any travel-related activities of prospective student-athletes and men's basketball coaching staff;

Maintain a comprehensive knowledge of the rules and regulations governing intercollegiate athletics competition and ensure strict compliance within the overall program, including without limitation NCAA and bylaws and Big Ten Conference regulations, and fully participate and cooperate in compliance-related activities, procedures and evaluations of the University;

Maintain an environment in which the coaching staff complies with NCAA rules and regulations "

This list of responsibilities is followed by Section 2.02 which states "Without limiting University's rights as otherwise set forth in the Employment Agreement, if the Employee is found to be in violation of any NCAA regulation, the Employee shall be subject to disciplinary or corrective action as set forth in the provisions of the NCAA enforcement procedures, including suspension without pay or termination of employment for significant repetitive violations."

Section 2.02 seems to sum it up pretty well for me. If you break the rules we can fire you. But they don't just leave it there. They get more detailed in the reasons they can fire him for cause.

"It is recognized that certain limited circumstances may make it appropriate for the University to end this Agreement prior to completion of its entire term." There were two subsections under section 6.02 of Sampson's contract. Subsection A says (and I'm paraphrasing here) we don't have to pay you no more if, through circumstances natural or unnatural, you find yourself in the condition of not being alive anymore. Seems fair.

Subsection B seems to be the one that deserves our focus. It says, "The University shall have the right to end this Employment Agreement for just cause prior to its normal termination on June 30, 2013. The term 'just cause' shall include, in addition to and as examples of its normally understood meaning in employment contracts, any of the following:

A significant, intentional, or repetitive violation of any law, rule, regulation, constitutional provision, bylaw, or interpretation of the University, the Big Ten Conference, or the NCAA, which violation may, in the sole judgment of the University, reflect adversely upon the University or its athletic program, including but not limited to any significant, intentional, or repetitive violation which may result in the University being placed on probation by the Big Ten Conference or the NCAA and including any violation which may have occurred during any prior employment of the Employee at another NCAA member institution and for which the NCAA could hold the Coach responsible;

A significant, intentional, or repetitive violation of any law, rule, regulation constitutional provision, bylaw, or interpretation of the University, the Big Ten Conference or the NCAA by a member of the intercollegiate men's basketball coaching staff or any other person under the Employee's supervision and direction, including student athletes in the program, which violation the Employee knew or should have known of and which violation may, in the sole judgment of the University, reflect

206

adversely upon the University and its athletic program, including but not limited to any significant, intentional, or repetitive violation which may result in the University being placed on probation by the Big Ten Conference or the NCAA;

A failure to maintain an environment in which the coaching staff complies with NCAA, Big Ten and University rules and regulations;

A failure to comply with Article VII of the Agreement regarding Unique Services; knowingly misleading the University about any matters related to the men's basketball program, its assistant coaches or student athletes.

Findings of the NCAA infractions committee referenced in Section 4.08 that demonstrate serious intentional or repetitive violations and that result in additional significant penalties or sanctions against the Employee beyond the University of Oklahoma's self-imposed sanctions taken against the Employee, including any action of the NCAA that would materially impair the Employee's ability to perform under this Agreement."

It seems that any or all of those applied to this situation and could have been just cause to terminate his contract and not pay him one more cent, but it also seems I'm wrong about that.

People smarter than me who were hired to find the holes in contracts like this must have found enough little cracks that made the university think that if they tried to fire him for cause before the hearing in front of the NCAA Committee on Infractions in June, he would sue them and possibly cost them a lot of money, so they were left with three options:

Fire him for cause and take your chances that if he sues, you can get it dismissed quickly and for minimal legal fees.

Fire him without cause, which would require you to pay him the remainder of his contract.

Negotiate a buyout for considerably less than either option one or two would have cost getting him to agree not to sue, which of course is exactly what they did

It bums me up that you can do what he did to this program and walk away with $750,000 dollars. There should have been a real consequence for Sampson. There were surely going to be consequences for the players, the program, the university, and the fans.

So, that's how I reacted. How the players reacted was much more important and sadly, much more telling. Prior to the press conference announcing Sampson's fate, the players and coaches were informed of the decision and with a game the next day, Head Coach Gerald Ford, sorry Dan Dakich, held practice.

Well, he tried to hold practice but Ray McCallum was meeting with Rick Greenspan, presumably trying to figure out how it is that the university hired a guy who'd been on a boat for the last five years. You can hold an effective practice two coaches down, but you know what makes it really hard? Being six players down.

DJ, DeAndre the Giant, McGee, Crawford, Bassett, and Elllis all skipped practice fueling rumors that they would also boycott the trip to Northwestern and possibly the rest of the season in protest of their coach getting fired [82] Debate raged among fans about how Dakich should

[82] I know. He wasn't "fired" but he was fired.

handle this situation, with many people calling for him to suspend them all.

There were calls from many corners for the type of discipline that people thought Knight would have brought to the situation. There were calls from other corners to bring Knight back to dispense whatever discipline was needed. After all, he was recently unemployed.

I understood the players' reaction. They had all come to IU to play for Sampson (or Davis) and now, after playing their guts out for him these past three games to gain a spot atop the Big Ten standings, he had been fired. They felt betrayed and like they needed to exert whatever power they had to let it be known that they were pissed. If only they'd thought to tell people to make sure their iced tea was exactly where they left it when they came back the next day, that might have been a big enough display of their power.

They were pissed at the university for firing Sampson. They were pissed at the media for calling for it. They were pissed at the NCAA. They were probably even pissed at the fans. But they didn't seem to be pissed at the one person who should be the target of all their anger.

They were angry, confused and acting completely out of emotion. In circumstances like this, you give kids a bit of a pass. And that's what Dakich did. He didn't suspend them all for missing that practice. The players didn't boycott anything. They were all there the next day, ready to board the plane for Northwestern, if not exactly ready to play the game.

We struggled early in the season to play up to Knight's ratio of mental: physical = 4:1. We never quite made it. The Northwestern game was the biggest test of our progress toward 4:1 that we'd had all season. We weren't any worse physically than when we played Northwestern at the beginning of February at Assembly Hall. That game was played right after the back-to-back losses against UConn and Wisconsin and right before I started hating Illinois. Coming, as it did, after those two losses and before the trip to Illinois the first meeting was a challenge to the mental part of our game, but nothing like this. It was an island in the middle of a sea of craziness and the last home game we played prior to finding out for sure what we'd already suspected about Kelvin Sampson.

At the time Northwestern was 0-8 in conference and we were sitting pretty at 7-1. DJ posted a double-double of 26 and 13, while EJ hit 6-10 three-pointers and 7-8 free throws on his way to a game high 29 points.

Northwestern's offense of constant movement and back cuts caused us a lot of problems until we switched to a zone and held them scoreless for nine minutes. It wasn't a perfect game, but we hadn't played a perfect game all season. The last two had been as close as we'd come and while our talent level had not declined since Tuesday's win over Purdue, with a stretch run to a Big Ten title on the line, we were about to test our character and mental toughness.

It was not what I would have hoped, but it was exactly what I should have expected. Leading up to the game I was running a segment of point-counterpoint in my head, trying to decide if I thought we should win at Northwestern. The argument went like this:

Point: Northwestern hasn't won a game yet in the Big Ten. That's good.

Counterpoint: This is a road game and even under ideal circumstances those are never easy.

Point: But this is Northwestern and not only is Welsh-Ryan a very small gym, but there are a lot of IU alumni in Chicago and they come out in force at Northwestern. It's as close as we can get to a home game on the road.

Counterpoint: That's crap and you know it. Besides, did you forget that we fired our coach yesterday?

Point: Yeah, I know, and that's going to play havoc with their heads, but on the other hand, Dakich was in charge of the game plan for this game, so the preparation didn't suffer.

Counterpoint: Yeah, except for the fact that we haven't practiced since the Purdue game. We were off Wednesday and Thursday and only seven players showed up to practice on Friday.

Point: Well, um, at least we're well rested?

Counterpoint: Jane, you ignorant slut!

I was deeply divided, as you can probably tell. The fans in attendance were as well. There were enough IU fans in attendance to make "GO IU!" heard on TV, but there was one girl in the stands with a sign reading "Thanks Kelvin! Go IU!" I assume the first part of that was meant to be facetious.

Dakich received a rousing ovation from the crowd when he walked out on the court, but the Northwestern faithful took advantage of timeouts to chant "Where is Kelvin?" I assume that was rhetorical.

We started the game in the 2-3 zone, presumably with the thinking that it worked really well last time. Sadly, it did not work as well this time around, thanks in large part to Northwestern forward, Kevin Coble, who shot 5-6 from three-point range, 8-8 from the line and 12-16 overall for 37 points.

We started slow, which was not new for this team. We switched defenses and nothing seemed to work. We gave up open layups, couldn't stop dribble penetration and didn't close out well on three-point shooters.

Northwestern is a difficult team to play against. They are the only team that plays the way they do in the Big Ten. They spread the floor on offense, pull almost everyone up above the free throw line, and backdoor cut until they get an open layup or a defensive shift that opens up a shooter. The setup is relatively simple, but the execution is so good that it's hard to defend, especially if the defense does the same stupid things over and over. The point guard dribbles toward the wing where a Northwestern player is standing. When the ball gets closer to the wing player, his defender steps toward the ball and into the passing lane. As soon as the defender takes that step the wing man cuts backdoor for a layup. They do it often and they do it well. And the way we consistently tried to defend it was to overplay the wing, opening up the cutting lane more and not dropping to help on the cutter quick enough. It's maddening because not only does it work, but it also makes you look stupid. And stupid we did look.[83]

Our offensive was a horse of a different color. DJ posted yet another double-double with 16 and 11. Bassett led all Hoosier scorers with 24, trailed closely by Crawford who hung 21 on the Wildcats. EJ struggled from the field going only 2-6, but his 13-16 free throw shooting made the difference for him and his 18 total points.

---

[83] Me fail English? That's unpossible!

The emotional side of this game cannot be overstated. Most of the players came out with KS written on their shoes in a show of support for the person who got them into this situation in the first place. All of the pent-up emotion of the last few days came to a head with 14:21 to go in the second half. After fighting back to tie the game at 52-52 on a free throw by DJ, Crawford was fouled hard by guard Craig Moore, and wanted to be his huckleberry. DJ managed to calm Crawford down, but no one thought to calm down Ellis, who got involved and ran his mouth. He picked up a technical, looked like a lunatic, could not be calmed down, and had to sit.

Ellis sat until just under nine minutes left, and he was back in the game for only moments when he was stripped of the ball by guard Michael Thompson and his thoughtful and considered response was to try to tackle Thompson. His total lack of emotional control led to his fourth foul and the impression that he was clinically insane.

With a one-point lead, the ball, and 13 seconds on the clock, EJ traveled, committing our 17th turnover of the night and giving Northwestern the chance to win the game. Michael Thompson drove all the way to the basket, but DJ got his hand on the shot, secured the ball, and made two free throws to give IU a three-point lead and the win at 85-82.

We bent against Northwestern, but thanks to a blocked shot by DJ with five seconds to go and the subsequent two foul shots he made, we did not break. We pulled out a three-point win under the most difficult circumstances, giving Dakich a win in his first game as Indiana head coach.

It looked like this team, which had been tested by injuries, suspensions and coaching upheaval, had hardened themselves and come together to finish out the season strong. In order to win the Big Ten, this team was going to have to show great toughness and character and despite our difficulties on the defensive end and Ellis' election as Mayor of Crazy Town, toughness is what they showed in holding on to beat Northwestern.

From the almost home crowd environment at Northwestern, and that's not really accurate, that game was more like an IU v UK crowd in Freedom Hall; equally loud for both teams. We returned home to play against Ohio State. With two weeks left to go in the conference season IU, Purdue, and Wisconsin were tied atop the Big Ten standings with two losses each.

With four games to go we needed four wins to secure a share of the Big Ten title, and while we picked up a tough road win at Northwestern, no one was feeling very secure in this team's emotional health in the wake of Hurricane Kelvin.

Thanks in large part to Bassett's third great scoring game in a row we were able to win the first of those four games when Ohio State came to Bloomington. Bassett shot almost 64 percent from the field to lead the team in scoring with 23, while EJ struggled again from the field and only managed 17 points.

EJ's shooting had been much less consistent since he injured his left hand prior to the first Wisconsin game. He had games like the first Northwestern game where he shot 8-14 from the field and 6-10 from three, but the Purdue game began a slump he wouldn't pull out of. Against Purdue he shot 4-12 and 1-3 from three. He took half as many shots at Northwestern and made exactly half as many from the field, but his 1-5 night from behind the arc was the real issue. If he hadn't continued to shoot free throws his slump would have been much more

214

noticeable. His shooting got even worse in this Ohio State game as he went 1-8 from three. And to make matters worse he began to turn the ball over, giving it up seven times.

The lone bright spot in this mess was the consistent play of DJ, who fought through some cramping and leg pain in the second half to just miss another double-double with 16 and 8. He continued to have a stellar senior season. His level of performance, despite suffering through injuries, never dipped. Early in the season it looked like he would never find his way to leading this team, but from the Xavier game on, he was the unquestioned leader and the Big Ten MVP.

This game never felt as comfortable as the game in Columbus, but it's hard to tell whether we played that much worse, or whether I was projecting my unease onto the team. The game in Columbus never felt in doubt, despite the fact that we only won by six. This game felt very tight the whole time, even though we held a 13 point lead late in the first half. Ohio State fought back in the second half, but was never able to take the lead. When they got close, we got a basket or two and put a little space between the two teams.

It was another win, but with three games left to play, I was feeling less comfortable than I had all season. Still, there were only three to go and we were still in position to claim our first Big Ten Title since 2002.

The dictionary in the guts of my computer defines "character" as "strength and originality in a person's nature." The dictionary in the guts of my computer also defines "character" as "an interesting or amusing individual." The Wolf says, "Of course, because you *are* a character, does not mean you *have* character."

Even before the mutually-agreed-upon-don't-let-the-door-hit-you-on-the-ass-while-you-leave-here-with-750,000-of-my-dollars-and-would-you-also-like-to-screw-my-wife-while-you're-at-it Kelvin Sampson deal, I'd been wondering which of those definitions applied to this team.

Usually going through something difficult can build character in a person or a group. And this team had gone through a number of difficult times and come out the other side victorious. We played through a six-game stretch early with either Bassett or Crawford suspended. We played and easily dispatched Kentucky without EJ. We overcame our own inability to walk and chew gum at the same time at Minnesota, winning despite turning the ball over 26 times. We went into Illinois and pulled out a win against one of the nastiest crowds I've ever seen that wasn't throwing snowballs at Santa Claus. We played our three best games of the year with the immediate specter of Kelvin Sampson's dismissal hanging over our heads. But none of that could have prepared us for the challenge of actually moving forward after Sampson was ousted.

And that's when the real test of character began. Because after all of that I still wasn't sold that this team had character. I'd just seen too many examples of mistakes made early that were never corrected. This didn't seem to be a team that had really improved over the course of the season.

After the Northwestern game I started to think we had character. It was an ugly win, but we found a way to get it done. The Ohio State game was no help either way. We won. It wasn't a great game for us, but it wasn't like we lucked our way into a win in spite of ourselves.

Then we went to Michigan State. It was only two weeks since we beat the crap out of the Spartans in Assembly Hall. In those two weeks, one would think that the shock would have become less of a factor and a level of comfort would have settled in with this team. Dakich and Fish discussed that very thing prior to the game.

One would have been wrong. Boy, that escalated quickly. I mean that really got out of hand fast. DJ missed two layups and two free throws and Stemler picked up two quick fouls on the way to Michigan State building an eight point lead. We briefly cut it to five after a Bassett three-pointer, but the Spartans ran off six unanswered points forcing Dakich to burn a timeout with only 24 seconds to go until the TV timeout. Less than a minute after that timeout, Raymar Morgan hit a layup to give them the lead 20-10. It was Michigan State's eighth basket in 10 attempts.

Two more misses from EJ and one from DJ combined with five more points for MSU and with 13:18 to go in the first half we were down 25-10 and the game was over. By halftime MSU was up 59-31 as we rolled over like dogs. The game ended with an embarrassing score of 103-74.

It was a terrible defensive effort. We posted enough points to win on a lot of nights, but not when you let the other team do whatever they want whenever they want.

Maybe I was feeling defeatist at this point in the season, or maybe I knew all along that this was who we were, but I never felt a sense of confidence and comfort after any of our wins and after this loss I knew with an absolute certainty that we were done.

We bounced back on Senior Night against Minnesota posting another victory, but with the Michigan State loss we gave up our say in the Big Ten title. We were forced to hope for Wisconsin to lose, but it didn't matter because a Big Ten champion does not lose 103-74. We were characters without character and the worst was yet to come.

Interlude: Kyle Taber in the House

On March 30, 1981, a delusional man who had fallen in love with Jodie Foster found what was, in his broken mind, the perfect way to express his love for her. He just knew that if he shot and killed President Ronald Reagan she would go all gushy and be his forever lover. There were at least two flaws in his plan: First, while it's true that her character had a connection with Travis Bickel (pre-Mohawk), in real life she was far less involved with psychopaths. Second, she would have had to be ultra-turned on by his actions to overcome her lesbian tendencies. These hurdles were likely too large to clear, but he gave it his best shot anyway. Reagan was caught by a bullet that ricocheted off the limousine door and went under his left arm, but it was not enough to kill him.

Jodie Foster was impressed, but not won over.

This was front page news. It was the first attempt on a sitting American president's life since, Charles Manson family member, Squeaky Fromme pulled a loaded gun on Gerald Ford six years earlier, which, in retrospect, wasn't really that big a gap between assassination attempts. It was front page, above the fold, news.

Everywhere but Bloomington, Indiana.

The front page of the Bloomington *Herald-Telephone* ran two headlines the next morning. "Hoosiers - NCAA champs" and "Reagan Condition 'excellent' after surgeons remove bullet" in that order.

The President was shot and it didn't rate above the fold status because a much bigger story happened that same day.

Kyle Taber is exactly like Ronald Reagan.

At the beginning of the season, as I was taking my notes during the games, I was, as I often am, fascinated by the guys at the end of the bench who never see the court. I've long relished hitting that moment, late in the game, after the outcome of the game is no longer in doubt, when the walk-ons hit the court. Whenever Taber would hit the court in the waning moments I would mark his entrance to the game by writing kyle taber in the house! in my notes.

Taber kept this role until, realizing that a revolving door of Mike White, Stemler, and DeAndre the Giant at the four spot was not going to ever deliver the results he desired. Kelvin Sampson put Kyle Taber in the starting lineup against Northwestern. Taber played very well and, more than any of those other players could say, he played within his role. He went from my own private joke to starter and holder of serious minutes overnight.

He didn't start the next game at Illinois, but he entered the game less than four minutes into it. He returned to the starting lineup at Ohio State and Wisconsin, played significant minutes against Michigan State, started against Purdue, and on and on. Once he went from benchwarmer to the regular rotation he never went back. He never lit it up on the scoreboard or stuffed the stat sheet, but he played the exact kind of basketball an IU fan likes to see. He played hard, knew his role, and left it all on the court.

It was a tremendous success story that would have been an A1 story above the fold under any other circumstances.

Chapter Thirteen: I'm Flaming Rome, I'm Out

Every great sports movie you've ever seen is about the athlete or the team overcoming great adversity to find success or redemption. It's why sports movies are made. If people just wanted to watch one team play another with nothing on the line they'd watch baseball. In July. All the time.

But if you're going to turn a sports story into a book, or a movie, or a movie based on a book, or a TV show based on a movie based on a book[84] it has to have more drama than that. There has to be more at stake.

In *Rocky* it was the true underdog story. Just standing in and fighting against the champ, fighting against insurmountable odds, was enough. And it was a theme Stallone returned to in *Rocky Balboa*. In between, Rocky needed to fight to overcome the feeling that he was a ~~sideshow act. Losing to the champ~~ wasn't enough to get him the respect

[84] Friday Night Lights I'm looking in your direction.

he always wanted. He needed to fight to prove to himself that he had been a true champion and hadn't been carried by his manager. He had to fight to avenge the death of a friend and to defeat communism. And he had to fight, in the middle of the street, for no reason I can remember.[85]

Daniel Laruso had to fight to stand up to bullies and prove that he belonged. He had to fight to defend the honor of a girl and bring two old friends back together again. He also had to fight from becoming Evil Laruso with a goatee for other reasons I don't remember.[86]

The Hickory Huskers had to win for all the small schools that never got to be there. They had to win for their drunk assistant coach drying out in the hospital. They had to win for the redemption of the coach who lost everything in one momentary loss of control.

The *Mighty Ducks* had to win so Disney could get a toe hold in the NHL.

Danny Noonan had to win to avoid working in a lumber yard and because he had to go to college.

Ray Kinsella had to plow under his cornfield to build a baseball diamond so he could have a catch with his father.[87]

The Rockford Peaches had to win to heal the rift between two sisters, bring the boys home, emancipate women, and keep Madonna's bosoms from popping out.

---

[85] And as much as I like being accurate I will not sit through Rocky V again, and you can't make me.

[86] See above note about Rocky V and apply it to Karate Kid III.

[87] Also because he was the biggest horses ass in three counties, seemingly.

There were larger things at stake and there were obstacles to overcome. The fact that they overcame these obstacles is why there were movies made about them. No one writes books or makes movies about a team that gave up and limped to the finish line just wishing for the season to be over so they could get on with the business of not going to class and failing drug tests. Until now.

Between the bounce back against Minnesota on Senior Night and the road game at Penn State the next Sunday, our hopes of a Big Ten title were dashed. Wisconsin beat Northwestern on Saturday to clinch the title. A win at Penn State was needed to lock up second place in the regular season and secure that spot in the Big Ten tournament.

Ellis did not make the trip to Happy Valley for the game for undisclosed disciplinary reasons, bringing the number of players suspended for at least one game this season up to three.[88] First Bassett, then Crawford, and now Ellis. This is another Kyle Taber/Ronald Reagan situation. Had it not been for the fact that we fired our coach mid-season for cheating and lying, the fact that we had three different players suspended over the course of the season should have raised red flags for everyone, but I guess by this point I had come to expect stuff like this. If we weren't injured or turning the ball over 26 times, or lying down like dogs in East Lansing, we were playing short-handed because of suspensions.

We were playing a road game with nothing at stake and short-handed one week after playing our last road game where we didn't even bother to show up. We were playing a team that was also short-handed, boasted a six-win conference season and was a terrifying 14-15 overall.

---

[88] Four, if you count AJ Ratliff missing the entire first semester as academically ineligible.

Oh yeah, and they were a team we had beaten by 16 in January.

It was a ridiculously even game. Penn State had a six-point lead at one point in the first. We had an eight-point lead once in the second. We shot 38 percent from the field. They shot 37 percent. We outshot them from the line 76 percent to 55 percent. We out rebounded them by five. But we turned the ball over 17 times to their eight and EJ couldn't get a jumper to fall at the end of regulation or a game-tying three to fall late in overtime, or almost anything else. EJ concluded his season in a massive slump by shooting a woeful 8-24 including 4-16 from three. We lost to Penn State by four in overtime to end the up-and-downiest regular season I had ever seen.

We went from 16 points better than Penn State at home in January to four points worse on the road in March, which was sadly reminiscent of the horrific turnaround from 19 points better than Michigan State to 29 points worse.

It was clear that I was not about to witness a great story of perseverance and dedication. This wasn't going to be the team that overcame early season struggles and a late season coaching change, relied upon each other and fought valiantly to restore the honor of a program tarnished by the actions of one incredibly selfish person. I would have liked to have seen that movie. I even know someone who could have written the script.

This was going to be the team that gave up.

It's a strange thing, giving up. Giving up in an individual sport is easy. It's an act that takes only a second and is completed in one action. Wrestlers can tap out and the match is over. Golfers can walk off the course and withdraw from the event and their day is over. Marathon runners can just start walking. Giving up as a member of a team is completely different.

It takes a whole team to win, but if a few people on the team quit, the whole team suffers through it, and what's worse is you still have to play the entire game and the entire schedule. It's brutal to watch and I'm sure even more brutal to be a part of, especially if you're one of the ones who still cares.

It was clear that Sampson's departure had sucked the life out of this team. Teams they had beaten handily were now beating them, and with each successive defeat the likelihood of future wins got smaller.

After the loss at Penn State, Purdue picked up a win securing them second in the Big Ten and dropping us to third where we were set for a rematch against Minnesota, a team we just beat handily on Senior Night. If I had the ability to pull back from the situation and see the patterns at play, I would have been certain of a loss against Minnesota, but when I'm in the moment with IU basketball I view every game we suit up for as a chance to win the game. I looked at the Minnesota game and said, "I like Dustin Hoffman and Warren Beatty. I bet if you put them in a desert something interesting will happen."

Something interesting happened alright, but before we get to that, it should be noted that at the end of the regular season DJ was named Big Ten Player of the Year, EJ was named Big Ten Freshman of the Year and Bassett was named to the third-team All-Big Ten Team. I hope these players were proud of these accomplishments. They earned them. But it's hard for me to feel good about individual player accomplishments, no matter how well deserved when the team takes a nosedive like this team did.

Prior to the game Fish and Leary had the same conversation that we've all heard countless times about how hard it is to beat a team for the third time in a season. I'm calling shenanigans on that. I'm going to say it's harder to beat a team that has beat your brains in twice already in a year. If you've beat them twice, you are the better team and have shown that you can do it. Twice.

It is, however, hard to beat a team that you've beaten twice when prior to the third meeting your team has given up.

That's not to say our entire team had given up. I don't think there's any give up in DJ. EJ was a fighter. And Taber had shown himself to be a tough and committed player, but not everyone has to give up for it to hurt the team. One guy giving up, or just not going full out, slows your defensive rotation, slows your hustle, and can help give the other team the confidence they need to outplay you. It only took three players to shave points and dump a game for Kentucky.

DJ certainly fought all the way to the end. Not only did he lead both teams in scoring and rebounding, he was center stage at the end of the game fighting to secure us the win.

With Minnesota leading 57-55 with 24 seconds remaining, Tubby Smith called a timeout to set up one play that would give Minnesota a two possession lead and hand Indiana the ball back with under 15 seconds remaining. The play worked like a charm, freeing Dan Coleman for a layup with 13 seconds on the clock. A made layup would have sealed Indiana's fate, but DJ came over and blocked he shot, and Ellis grabbed the rebound, securing the ball for IU and a chance to tie the game.

Dakich got a timeout with 10.6 seconds to go, with a chance to set up one play to force overtime. At this point in the game we were 1-14 from three-point range, making an Eric Gordon drive to the basket the single best option on the table. EJ brought the ball the length of the floor and got fouled as he drove the lane with 3.4 seconds to go. He missed the first free throw, forcing him to intentionally miss the second. In a play that almost never works, DJ got the rebound on the miss, tipped it back in and got fouled. The game was tied at 57 with 3.1 seconds on the clock with DJ on the line to give us a one-point lead. It felt like we might be able gut out a win after a long game where we shot 32% from the field and 67% from the line, but DJ missed the free throw. As the rebound bounced back long the hope that I had allowed to build up inside me, yet again, was dashed, until DJ came up with the rebound! And was fouled.

Despite watching a team that had largely given up on themselves and the season, the basketball gods were not allowing me to give up on one last win. DJ went back to the line and missed the first free throw. This was getting ridiculous. But he made the second to put us ahead by 1 with 1.5 seconds and the length of the floor to go for Minnesota.

Tubby Smith called a timeout to set up what would be at best a desperation heave. Hoffarber, a player who won an ESPY in high school for making a game-winning basket at the buzzer while sitting on the ground, grabbed the pass just above the free throw line and threw up a runner that went in just as time expired. This drove whatever hope was left in the Indiana fans, and whatever fight was left in the Indiana players, rushing out of them.

I have never seen a game with so many "what-ifs" packed into the last five seconds. In the last 3.4 seconds of a two-point game we missed four of five free throws. If EJ had made the first two we would have been tied and Minnesota would have had more time to run a play for the last shot. If DJ had completed the three-point play we would have had a one-point lead with longer to defend than we ultimately had, and it's very

226

possible Minnesota could have gotten an even better look with 3.1 than they got with 1.5. If DJ had made both of those final two free throws instead of just one the best Hoffarber could have done with that exact same shot was to tie the game.

It was an amazingly complicated 3.4 seconds and, had we played a better game up to that point, 3.4 seconds that may never have happened, but we missed a lot of free throws and Hoffarber hit a very hard shot.

Self-inflicted wounds and big shots by our opponents devastated this team, and now there was but one game left in the most incomprehensible season of Indiana basketball ever. At this point in the season I found myself, like Homer, standing on the overpass after Lisa ruined my picnic by shoving the grill with the pig on it down the street, necessitating that I chase it as it rolled through the bushes.

It's just a little dirty. It's still good. It's still good as it jumped a bridge and landed in the river. *It's just a little slimy. It's still good. It's still good,* until it got plugged in the drainpipe, causing a pressure build up that launched it through the sky. As I watched the pig sail by overhead I turned to anyone who would listen to my half-hearted pleas that this season (like the pig that had come to represent it) was *just a little airborne. It's still good. It's still good.* The response I got was a deafening, *It's gone.* The only retort I could muster was a very weak, *I know.*

I watched Selection Sunday with an interesting emotional mix that can be best described as trepidation combined with anger, resignation, and a dash of just wanting this whole thing to be over. But, as with most things in my IU life, I erred on the side of self-delusion. Despite our ridiculous collapse and predilection of late to either lose by a lot to teams we recently beat by a lot, or lose close games to other teams we also recently beat by a lot, I knew we were talented enough to justify a four seed. There wasn't a team in the country that an early-February version of this team couldn't beat. Sadly, there wasn't a team in the country that this mid-March version could expect to beat.

And while the committee gets a lot of things wrong a lot of the time, and despite my protestations to the contrary at the time, they got it right when they gave us an eight seed and pitted us against Arkansas in the first round.

A season spent rooting against the better angels of my nature had left me exhausted and desirous of a merciful ending to this mess. Enough members of this team had already quit. I didn't want to join their ranks, but deep inside, in places I don't talk about at parties, I was ready to quit too.

One of the lessons I have carried with me from childhood, one instilled in me by my father during my last season as a borderline mediocre little league baseball player, was that it isn't okay to quit things.

I wasn't having any fun sucking at baseball anymore. I was no longer sustained by the occasional duck snort or error-induced arrival at first base and I felt I had contributed all I could in the area of dandelion picking. I wanted to quit, but I was told that I had made a commitment and I had to see it through. If I didn't want to play next year, that was fine, but I was not allowed to quit.

I have never lost the dislike of quitting things. But I also learned later in life that in America when we don't like our jobs we don't go on strike, we just go in every day and do it really half-assed.

I'd spent the entire season striking balances. I struck a balance between sticking to my beliefs about doing things the right way and my desire for this team to win. So, it wasn't difficult to strike the precarious balance that served me well during February and March of 2008. I'd been compromising myself for months, why stop now? I didn't quit cheering for the Hoosiers, but I did it really half-assed.

The universe, however, was not done pouring rubbing alcohol over the cuts on the back of my legs. After being forced to endure the biggest quality drop-off since season six of the *X-Files*, and facing what was likely the rifle barrel through the slats of Old Yeller's cage, I wasn't able to just cower in the back of my cage, waiting for my best friend to pull the trigger on my rabid ass. I had to sit there and stare down the barrel of the gun while Billy Packer gave me the color commentary.

It's not enough that I was in a position where I was cheering for a team I had lost all hope in. It wasn't enough that we went from 17-1 and atop the Big Ten standings to losers of three of our last four with two of those losses coming against Penn State and Minnesota, who, and I don't know if I mentioned this before, we had beaten badly earlier in the season, and in one case beaten in their gym despite turning the ball over 26 times. It wasn't bad enough that after the worst season in my entire life (the 14-15 campaign of 2004) I had to sit through the marginally better 15-14 2005 season. It wasn't bad enough that we then hired a guy who didn't just have a history of NCAA violations, but was under sanctions at the time we hired him. It wasn't enough that he couldn't find it within himself to not immediately do the exact same thing he was being sanctioned for doing. It wasn't enough that the one thing we, as IU fans could always rely on, our absolute certainty that no matter what you wanted to say about Hoosier basketball we could always say that we had done things the right way, had been taken from us. It wasn't enough that through one terrible hire and a complete failure to monitor the actions of a known cheater we had given up the high moral ground and were now on the level of UK. No, those things added together weren't enough. I had to suffer through this while Billy Packer called the game! Why didn't they just kick me in the balls and tell me I had ugly children?[89]

In a season of strange, the final game fit right in. It was the usually spot on Jim Nance who provided the head-scratching comments to start this game. Prior to the game, in what I assume was an homage to the Kelvin Sampson method of beginning a sentence and forgetting halfway through it how that sentence began, Nance gave us the "either but" question. "Will it be the team that started the season 17-1, but lost three of their last four?" The answer, sadly, was yes.

But my favorite Nance moment of the game came after Arkansas guard Stefan Welsh rolled his ankle after coming down on Bassett's foot. Billy Packer said, "How often do you see that?"

"Almost every time." Nance replied.

That's right, almost every time someone jumps they roll their ankle by landing on an opponent's foot. It's so sad. You'd think they'd quit jumping, as dangerous as it is.

But Billy brought it all back home and reset the equilibrium when he said that "players don't want to get hurt this time of year," meaning either that there is a time of year that players would love to get hurt, or that while *players* might not want to get hurt this time of year, there is a group of people who spend the other 11 months of the year just waiting for March so they can get hurt.

---

[89] The answer is the same as Mike Tyson's when he was asked if he felt bad about saying that he was going to eat Lennox Lewis's children, praise be to Allah. "No, because he doesn't have children." At least at the time I didn't.

But the inexplicable didn't end in the broadcast booth. Dan Dakich got the single dumbest technical foul in the history of basketball when, at the 16:15 minute mark of the first half, with the game tied at seven, Dakich received a technical foul for refusing to give the ball back to the ref. The ball went out of bounds, Dakich picked it up, and when the ref reached for it, Dakich moved the ball out of his reach and took a shot for no reason at all.

There were two things, however, that anyone could have predicted. The first, sadly, was the continued horrible shooting by EJ. Since Sampson's departure EJ's ability to shoot the ball went away completely, making only 7-50 from three-point range. His numbers masked this slump as he continued to get to the line and score well from there, but his field goal percentage dropped considerably over that time period. He finished the Arkansas game with only eight points on 3-15 shooting, his first single digit scoring effort since he missed the second half of the Tennessee State game with a back injury.

Some of this surely is attributable to his wrist injury, but the atmosphere in Bloomington since Sampson's ouster must have made the reception he received at Illinois seem calm, and we saw what that did to his performance in the first half of that game.

The other fact that we all should have seen coming was the magnificent performance by DJ in his final game as a Hoosier. DJ went for 22 and nine and tried single-handedly to make this team care enough to fight, but his Jedi mind tricks did not work on them. The force was not strong enough to overcome the character flaws and mental weakness of this team. It was like the whole team was Watto.

Arkansas built a seven-point lead at the half and calmly and patiently extended it to a 14-point final spread. It was yet another game with no heart, where the players on the courts seemed to have no interest in playing with one another, or for IU. And it left me glad that it was finally over.

Interlude Thirteen: Never Have So Many

In the spring of 1998 I took a class on coaching basketball that was taught by Bob Knight and Norm Ellenberger. It was mostly taught by Coach Ellenberger, but roughly every other class Coach Knight lectured on the value of hard work and education, how to get a job, professionalism, and sometimes basketball.

At the end of one class Coach Knight said that during the next class he would answer any question we had, provided it was an intelligent question. After watching one of my friends violate the only caveat in the whole process by asking Knight what he thought of the Big Ten tournament, to which Knight responded, "Where the hell have you been? Mars? Is there anyone in this room who can tell him my opinion of the Big Ten tournament?"[90] I got up my courage to ask about the increase of players going straight from high school to the pros and whether it was bad for college basketball.

Knight's response was that there weren't really that many players making that leap. Not satisfied with that answer, I reworded my question to work in that there is a perception created in the media that there are a large number of players jumping straight to the pros or leaving early. His response was to say this about the media, "Never have so many known so little about so much."

He didn't really give me the answer I was looking for, but at least I didn't feel like an ass for asking.

Prior to the Arkansas game it was announced that IU had formed a search committee to find the next coach, which fueled an already ongoing

---

[90] There was. Everyone. He didn't like it.

debate about who should be the next coach at IU. A debate backed by such facts as: *if IU wins the first two rounds of the NCAA they have to hire Dakich. Alford is the only answer. We should hire Jamie Dixon because Bob Knight thinks that Pitt should win the whole thing this year. And Thad Matta has shown he can recruit. I bet he'd jump from Ohio State to IU.*

It was weeks of rumor-fueled speculation that involved many IU fans taking extremely impassioned stands either for or against a coach who may or may not have ever been considered for the job. In other words, it was a lot of people getting themselves worked up into a shoot based on no actual information.

The same thing happens every year in recruiting, as people get emotionally invested in the decisions of 16- to 18-year-old boys who they have never met and based on math alone, will very likely never wear an Indiana uniform.

I'm not above this kind of nonsense. I'm still mad at Eric Montross and I have gone from intense love to near hatred of people like Luke Recker and Jason Collier.

No one knew anything about who our next coach was going to be. I'm certain at this point even our next coach didn't know he was going to be our next coach. But, in an age of message boards and the near anonymity of chat room usernames, not only does everyone have an opinion; they have a place to spew it. And if you don't have an opinion formed yet, you are more than welcome to go read other people's and tell them why they are stupid.

The truth is we're all idiots who should just shut up and pay attention once someone has been hired or suits up for IU. We'll save ourselves a lot of drama. And I, for one, was kind of done with drama for a while. Except, I wasn't anywhere near done with drama.

Chapter Fourteen: And Then There Was One

Kermit the Frog sat on a park bench in England, clutching a glass slipper to his chest. He looked crestfallen. A rumpled stranger approached, sat down next to him and said:

I see the way you're sittin' there. I see the way you've got your hand around that little shoe and that's all I need. I know your whole story. Well, I tell you friend, what happened was you and your brother-in-law, Bernie you cashed in your stock certificates and your insurance policy and you went out and bought a dry cleaning establishment. Now, another place opens up down the street and it's chargin' less and they're gettin' the stuff out faster because they got more help. It's not your fault! Right? Alright, so Bernie comes to you, he says, 'I want you to buy me out.' He says he's fed up. Well, your kids are growing up. You never see 'em. And all of a sudden they're turning into juvenile delinquents. And your wife is sayin' to you 'Look, you care more about this lousy business than you care about me.' And your equipment breaks down and your sister moves in because that jerk, Bernie, he went and joined the circus. Well, you had it up to here, right? You didn't know what to do. So what did you do? You did the only thing you could do. You dumped the business for a song. And who did you sell it to? You sold it to that jerk down the street, that slob that had been burying you for a year. Then, you took whatever money you had left and you sunk it into the glass slipper business.

That's your story my friend. Not a happy one is it?

And Kermit replied, "You know it's amazing. You are 100 percent wrong. I mean, nothing you've said has been right."

That's what we call being Peter Falk. It revolves around taking a small piece of information and forming from that a very involved and completely incorrect assessment of a situation. Being Peter Falk seemed to be catching in the spring of 2008.

As bad as the month between Sampson's ouster and the end of the season was, the next month was much, much worse. May you live in interesting times, indeed.

Kelvin Sampson had signed four recruits for the 2008-2009 class: Matt Roth, Tom Pritchard, Devin Ebanks, and Terrell Holloway. With all of the uncertainty surrounding the program and the fact that the coach they signed to play for was gone, Ebanks and Holloway asked for and received releases from their letters of intent before the season was even over. Pritchard and Roth remained in the fold, but with no coach in place for next year, their commitment to their commitment seemed far from certain.

DJ was set to graduate, as was Stemler, Adam Ahlfeld, Mike White, and the already departed AJ Ratliff. We had a roster of 13 scholarship athletes and after these graduations we were down to eight.

There were a number of people trying to make the case that it was in EJ's best interest to stay one more year because he had such a shooting slump toward the end of the year and that he would benefit from another year of development. I was making a similar argument. I was telling everyone who would listen, and even some who wouldn't, that it was in Jennifer Love Hewitt's best interest to come over to my house and get undressed.

While both of those arguments may end up benefitting EJ and Love in some way, they were fundamentally selfish arguments whose true meaning was that it would be in MY best interest if either of those things happened. Sadly, neither did.[91] EJ declared for the draft in early April.

And then there were seven. I did my own math on our returning players and here was my logic. Be prepared for some pretty well thought out Peter Falk. Ellis and DeAndre the Giant would be back. They were JuCo transfers with only one year of eligibility left. It would not be in their interest to leave at this point. Taber would be back for his senior season. He had been through three coaches to this point and had worked his way up to getting meaningful minutes I couldn't see a reason why he would go. He wasn't likely to find a better situation for himself than the one he already had. Holman had already lost an entire season to his injury. I couldn't see him voluntarily sitting out another one after transferring. Bassett might go. He could sit a year and still have two remaining. He would also likely be able to find himself a pretty good situation. Crawford could see the same picture Bassett sees and decide to look elsewhere.

McGee was, to my mind, the most likely to go. He seemed to have the raw talent to play elsewhere, but he was pretty far down on the depth chart after sitting the bench the entire season.

By my calculations we were looking at likely having four to six returning players, plus whatever recruits we could hold on to, and maybe a transfer or two who wanted to follow whomever our coach might be. It wasn't ideal, but it wasn't a horrible foundation upon which to start rebuilding.

Wow! It's amazing. You are 100 percent wrong. Others were lining up behind me to Peter Falk the hell out of the coaching search.

On April 1, 2008 the fine folks over at peegs.com updated their coaching hot board *shudder* with the headline "Top Three Emerging." Sources indicated to peegs that Sean Miller of Xavier, Anthony Grant of

---

[91] Yet.

Virginia Commonwealth, and Brad Brownell of Wright State were "the trio now standing out."

They didn't just pull that top three out of thin air. It was Peter Falked in the proper fashion. A small piece of information was turned into an incredibly inaccurate conclusion. From the time Sampson exited stage left the list of potential Hoosier coaches had grown, in no particular order, to include Thad Matta, Steve Alford, Dan Dakich, Mike Woodson, Norman Dale, Scott Skiles, John Calipari, Rick Pitino, Hayden Fox, Tom Crean, Tony Bennett, Emilio Estevez, Sean Miller, Brad Brownell, Anthony Grant, Ernie Pantusso, Isiah Thomas, Larry Bird,[92] Tony Bennett, Jamie Dixon, Rick Barnes, Bob Knight, Tom Izzo, and John Wooden.

Many intelligent, fact-based conversations were held between the fans, polls were taken, and a consensus leader had emerged. A poll was taken on March 26 to see who the fans had convinced themselves they wanted and the Indiana Universe spoke with one loud and disjointed voice. Tony Bennett was the guy we wanted. He had all the credentials we thought were important, like being a present coach who had success somewhere much smaller and nowhere near Indiana, and having held a long-term engagement at The Sands.[93]

Late in March the word spread that IU had offered the position to Bennett, who, after a conversation with Rick Greenspan called espn.com and told them he had "decided not to pursue the Hoosiers' head coaching job."

Panic was starting to spread. The season had been over for a whole

[92] He came for a few weeks, Kent Benson scared him off.

[93] Sorry. Had to pick the low-hanging fruit.

240

week and we hadn't hired the greatest coach in the history of basketball to be our next coach. And now it looked like the second best coach in the history of basketball, you know, the head coach at perennial powerhouse Washington State University, had turned us down.

We were despondent. In the eight days since the season ended, if the incredibly scientific polls could be believed, this is the guy we had always wanted. If he didn't want us, then who would? It's the same way I felt after my first girlfriend and I broke up.

We were insecure now. We started from the position that ours was the greatest job in college basketball, and now, with one rejection, we felt like we were undatable. So we lowered our expectations.

We'd asked out the head cheerleader and she turned us down, so names like Izzo, Matta, Pitino, and Calipari dropped from the hot board. Dropped, not because they were no longer interested, or because the university didn't want them, but because we were all certain that no one who was worth our love would ever love us in return.

On April 1, our new list, adjusted for inflation, was Brownell, Grant, and Miller, until later on April 1, when all the speculation ended and it was announced the next Indiana head basketball coach was going to be...

But let's not get ahead of ourselves. My Falkian scenario was about to take its first hit from stupid reality. On March 31, Dan Dakich did the right thing at the wrong time. Though he may or may not have known it at the time, it was his last day as IU men's basketball coach. He knew he wasn't going to be the coach next season and he did something that shocked pretty much everyone outside the program.

During his press conference following the loss to Arkansas, Dakich dropped a very cryptic bombshell that I dismissed as being a reference to all the things Sampson had been involved in. He was asked how surprised he was by everything that had happened this season.

He responded, "I have never seen anything like it. It's probably not over to tell you the truth. The season and games are over but there are a lot of things that have to occur within Indiana basketball or there are a lot of things that are not going to occur in Indiana basketball that need to occur here in the spring time. It is far from over." But he never said he was surprised.

He was then asked how he was going to approach the offseason.

"I haven't really thought about it," he said. "The way I'm going to approach it is until they tell me I am not coaching I am going to do the things that are necessary within this program. I am going to make the decisions that are necessary and the accountability that is necessary within the culture of the basketball program to ensure that whomever, me or anybody else, that becomes the basketball coach here has a good culture."

And finally, when given the chance to lobby for the job he said a lot of things, many of them rambling and disjointed, but he talked about the culture of IU being essential to the success of the program and said that "the culture right now lends itself to exactly what is going on here."

Dakich was telling us that there were things going on behind the scenes that we didn't know about that had to change for IU to be the kind of program we all expect it to be and that while he was coach he was going to try to fix as much as he could. It was everything we needed to know to brace ourselves for the storm on the horizon. But no one seemed to see this for the warning it was. It was as direct as he could be without getting into specifics.

The only move he made publicly to address these cultural issues, he did on his last day in office. Presidents often pardon criminals, as their last act in office so they can do what they think is right without having to deal with the backlash. Dakich went the other way. On his last day as head coach, Dakich kicked Bassett and Ellis off the team for missing a meeting and then for skipping the punishment they were given the next morning, at least this was the reason given at the time.

Both of these players had been suspended this season, so we knew there were larger problems backstage, and yet we were still surprised.

The reaction from the same fan base that wanted Dakich to suspend the six players who skipped practice on the day Sampson resigned was the exact opposite this time around. Who did he think he was? He wasn't going to be the coach next year, what right did he have to kick players off next year's team?

But none of us knew what was really going on behind the scenes, and we still don't completely. Dakich did what he thought was right for the good of the program. It's what he told us he was going to do while he was still coach. He was going to do what the program needed, not what was easiest for him.

Ok, so my prediction about Ellis was wrong, but I thought it was possible that Bassett wouldn't be back, so I was still backing my reasoned appraisal of our 2008-2009 roster. Besides, when we hired the next coach, maybe he'd reverse what Dakich did. I wasn't Falked just yet.

The coaching hot board, and everyone who thought they knew who the next coach was, also proved to be Peter Falk on April 1 when the university announced that the next head coach for the Indiana Hoosiers would be Tom Crean of Marquette. He must have been fourth on the hot list.

When Crean was announced the following day as the new head coach, one of the first things he did was hold up a T-shirt that he had been handed the night before when his plane landed at Monroe Country Airport. It was a red shirt with white lettering that said simply, Crean & Crimson.

Crean struck the right note from the start. He made it clear that he had roots in Indiana. His brothers-in-law Jim and John Harbaugh had Indiana ties, Jim as Colts QB and John as a coach under Cam Cameron. He spoke about his memories of the '76 championship, a picture of Kent Benson that hung on his wall as a kid, as well as his first coaching clinic away from home, which was run by Bob Knight. He was tapping into our tradition, possibly because he knew, even then, how much we'd have to rely on our good feelings of days gone by to get through the aftermath of he who shall not be named.

It's been a few years since Crean gave this press conference, and it still gives me chills to hear it because it felt like a cool breeze pushing its way through an open window. This press conference sits in a very brief window of hope between the disgust of the previous season and what we didn't know then, but were soon to find out.

Crean himself summed up all of this in a few words. He managed to say why he took the job, why what happened could never happen again, why we demand more of ourselves and our program, why we expect to win and to win the right way, why we expect our players to graduate, and why we won't compromise who we are anymore just to win.

He said, "It's Indiana. It's Indiana."

The first question Crean answered was about the challenge in recruiting for the next season and whether he would consider bringing back Ellis and Bassett. He wasn't able to give an answer, but indicated that the situation would be reviewed in the coming days and weeks.

We spent the next month wondering about recruits and player defections, with very little known. Crean decided to reevaluate the Bassett and Ellis dismissals, so we were still holding out some hope that whatever they had done to earn this dismissal could be remedied by a new coach.

The month of April provided few revelations. Pritchard and Roth confirmed their commitments. E̅ announced his intentions for the NBA, surprising no one. Ohio junior forward Bobby Capobianco became Crean's first commitment for the class of 2009. Crean picked up commitments from junior college transfer Devan Dumas and class of 2008 guard Nick Williams. Crean had started to build a roster to play the next season. But April showers brought May what-the-hells?!

On May 1, Holman surprised Coach Crean by asking for a transfer and surprised the office staff by rearranging the office by way of hurling a potted plant across the room in anger. The impetus behind Holman's decision to transfer was a sudden overwhelming urge to move to Detroit. The fact that Ray McCallum had just left IU to become the head coach there and lobbied Holman to come with him may have played a role, but I hear Detroit is lovely in the spring, so maybe not. The police were called to Assembly Hall in response to Holman's outbreak, but no arrests were made.

And then there were six.

The next morning Crean announced he was upholding the decision to get rid of Bassett and Ellis and he that he had dismissed DeAndre from the team and revoked his scholarship saying, "Our staff is going to ensure that anyone who attends this university and wears the Indiana uniform will make this privilege among their highest priorities and not treat the opportunity as an entitlement."

And then there were three.

It didn't end there. Three weeks later McGee was dismissed from the team for "academic and team guideline negligence." Crean had not only upheld what Dan Dakich had done, but after taking a month to evaluate the players in the program and the entire culture in place he came to the same conclusion Dakich had come to by the end of the season. This thing was broken and the only way to fix it was to tear it down and start from scratch.

And then there were two.

Let's recap very briefly. Four guys graduated, one left for the pros. AJ Ratliff spent half the year ineligible and then quit mid-season. Bassett, Ellis, McGee, and DeAndre were all kicked off the team and Eli went nuts and threw a potted plant across the office bringing the police into Assembly Hall.

What we can infer from this is that aside from the guys who either graduated or left for the NBA, Tom Crean felt there were three guys worth keeping around, Taber, Holman, and Crawford, and Eli left on his own.

The self-control it must have taken for Dan Dakich not to just unload with all of the things that were out of control with this program during that post-game press conference is truly remarkable.

The only two scholarship players that were left from the Kelvin Sampson era were Crawford and Taber, until the middle of June, when Crawford looked at the destruction all around him and decided he wanted no part of any of this. He transferred to Xavier. I can't say I blame him.

And then there was one.

Over the summer, the NCAA read our response and held their hearing. They agreed with us that the penalties we had imposed on ourselves were enough and that no more were warranted. They slapped Kelvin Sampson with the same penalty they gave to Dwane Casey in 1989. He was given a five year Show-Cause penalty. He then went to the NBA to be an assistant coach, once again following in Dwane Casey's footsteps.

In 1989 Kentucky was hit with three years probation, a two-year postseason ban, a one-year television ban, and a two-year reduction in scholarships after 18 major violations.

After five major violations in 2008, we imposed a scholarship restriction on ourselves. We never got a TV ban or a postseason ban, but our program was destroyed from within by a culture of leniency. With only one returning scholarship player and a two-man recruiting class we were in a position no major program had ever found itself in.

We had to start from scratch and the rebuilding process we would have to undergo would make Kentucky's look easy. We had our very own post-season ban. You don't make the NCAA tournament after your entire team either transfers, graduates, or is dismissed.

In their first year they were allowed back in the NCAA tournament, UK was a heart-breaking[94] buzzer beater by Christian Laettner away from beating Duke and advancing to the Final Four to play against us. That was 1992, three seasons after Eddie Sutton resigned and the NCAA put the hammer down on the Wildcats.

When you compare the transgressions, the responses, and the histories of the two programs it seems unjust that the rebuilding for Indiana would be so much harder than it was for Kentucky, but watching Alford sit out against UK in 1985 while they were being investigated for paying every player for 13 years, seemed unjust too, so it was consistent at least.

But it's that kind of thinking, blaming others and saying, "Yeah, but everyone is doing it!" that Kentucky fans do so well. What we do at Indiana is accept the consequences for what we allowed to happen and hold our heads high that even in our darkest hours we hold ourselves to a higher standard than that.

---

[94] For them. I loved it.

Postlude: Something Bigger Than Yourself

If someone had given me a cursed monkey's paw in October 2007, I couldn't have made any bigger mess out of things. I wished for a meaningful beginning. I wished for consistency. I got them both.

The way this season started told me everything I needed to know. The NCAA was going to investigate the program and this was a team that would use their athletic ability and talent to overcome defensive lapses, but they would never get any better. They would always be a bad defensive team. They would always get beat in transition and be slow to help.

Be careful what you wish for, you just might get it.

A few things were obvious to me at the end of this season. The first is that predictions are meaningless. The number of things I never saw coming numbered in the millions, even though all the evidence of their inevitability was right there for me to see. We were all surprised to lose to Xavier, but we had beaten lesser competition with subpar basketball up to that point. It was inevitable that we were going to stumble.

I was stubbornly holding on to my belief that this team was a top tier team up to Selection Sunday, even though I knew better. We didn't play anyone all year and when we did, we lost, with the exception of one Michigan State and one Purdue game. We lost to Xavier, UConn and Wisconsin twice, while beating the likes of Chicago State, Coppin State, and every lower tier Division I team from North Carolina.

I knew the NCAA was investigating us. I knew Kelvin Sampson's history, and yet I wasn't expecting the NCAA to come back with findings of five major violations.

I never expected Hoosier fans to cheer for Sampson after the findings were made public just because we won a couple of games, but we fervently defended every boneheaded thing Bob Knight did. He never cheated, but he yelled, he threw things, he berated the press, and called Daryl Thomas a pussy roughly 3,500 times in one year, in front of a reporter. And some of us still defend him as entertaining and eccentric.

I never expected to enter the cave on Dagobah where I encountered the wildcat mascot. Imagine my surprise when I cut its head off and found my face staring back at me. I knew how destructive hate could be. I knew about tempting fate and still I hate who they are and what they stand for, and faced with similar circumstances I found myself reacting in many of the same ways. I tried to have it both ways. I tried to root for my team and decry my coach, but before that I put all the cheating out of my mind for months and cheered unreservedly for my team.

In the end we did it. We walked right up to the precipice and peered into the Great Pit of Carkoon into the mouth of the Sarlacc where we would have learned a new meaning of pain and suffering as we were slowly digested over a 1,000 years. We looked into that abyss. And we turned away.

I was shocked, by the time that Crawford transferred and we started hearing things leaking out of the program like 19 Fs and 30 failed drug tests, how insanely close we all came to being Kentucky fans.

I always wondered as a kid, and still do, even more so as an adult, how people can support a program that is dirty. How you can put winning above everything else. I understand why Kentucky is that way. They've been that way for 60 years. Rupp's teams cheated. Joe B. Hall was a member of those teams, so his team's cheated, too. Cliff Hagan was also a member of those teams so when he was athletic director, he ran a dirty program and the fans from 1951 had kids who became the fans of 1978 and had kids of their own, each generation instilling in the next that the tradition at Kentucky was winning and that sometimes, to win, you needed to break the rules, because rules are for suckers. Because win = good and lose = bad. And anytime someone tells you how twisted and broken your school is, they're only saying things like that because they're jealous and besides, everyone else cheats, so what's the big deal.

The first step toward accepting that kind of behavior comes from the reaction of those in power when the first rules get broken. Rupp set the tone when he tried to excuse his former players' point shaving by saying, "Hey, all they did was shave points. They never threw a game." Every reaction from that moment forward was to blame everyone but the guilty party.

In 2008 our players tried to take that approach. When Sampson resigned they were mad at the world, but not at Sampson, at least not publicly. The fans in the stands seemed to forgive Sampson almost immediately because we beat Michigan State and Purdue. Who cares about phone calls? At least we never mailed $1,000 to our recruits.

Many members of the media weren't willing to stand up and call for a house cleaning. Dick Vitale being one big exception, a role he also played in 1989 when he called for the ouster of Eddie Sutton from Kentucky.

I never stopped rooting for this team, even when they had stopped rooting for themselves. I was disgusted at Sampson and his actions. I was mad at Rick Greenspan for steering the ship while all of this was going on, but I largely gave the players a pass. I figured it had to be hard on them to deal with all the distractions.

251

I had sold out my beliefs, or at least was willing to compromise them so I could be outraged and still cheer for my team.

We were all guilty.

What stopped us from becoming Kentucky was the reaction of the university when the Notice of Allegations came down in February. Instead of taking 90 days to respond, taking their case to the hearing in June, suing the newspapers to keep them from releasing the results of the investigation or the findings from the NCAA, waiting for a final ruling in September, and then firing Sampson for cause after a lengthy due process, they acted quickly, and paid a small price, $750,000, for our souls.

They also made two other crucial decisions that kept us from silently and without a struggle going over to the Dark Side. They appointed Dan Dakich as interim head coach and they hired Tom Crean.

Dakich started cleaning things up immediately and made the right decisions under difficult circumstances. He made accountability important again and started a process that Tom Crean continued.

It would have been much easier for Crean to reinstate Bassett and Ellis and to forgive the transgressions of those who brought home the 19 Fs and 30 failed drug tests. The next two seasons would have been much more successful and profitable for the university, but he chose the hard path. He chose to act because it's Indiana and it's important that we remain Indiana.

It never occurred to me how many of the players were part of a much deeper problem, a problem that was much more disturbing than recruiting violations and three-way phone calls.

Knowing now what I know, I'm glad they quit on us. I just think how I'd feel now if they'd won something.

I've spent so much of my life as a sports fan hating everything that UK stood for and holding up IU as the way a program should be run, and it turned out that I should have heeded what Yoda and Emperor Palpatine had been saying.

Hatred does lead to suffering. Fear and anger are of the Dark Side. When you give in to your hate and anger you begin your march down the path to the Dark Side.

By the end of that season I was rooting for a team that embodied everything I hated about UK. The coach was a cheater. The players were skipping and failing classes and many of them were on drugs. This was no longer Indiana.

I once saw Mike Powell, former IU wrestler and head wrestling coach at Oak Park River Forest High School in Illinois, speak to a group of eighth graders at their end of year athletic banquet. I was predisposed to like Mike, as he was a fellow Hoosier, but he was also a great speaker and he said something that hit home with me.

He said that he tells his wrestlers all the time how important it is to believe in something bigger than yourself, something from which you can draw strength and inspiration when you need it.

I believe in Indiana basketball.

I believe in all the players who have worn that uniform with pride and represented our school. I believe in winning with integrity and playing by the rules. I believe in finding success by doing things the right way. I believe in all of these things and that's why what Kelvin Sampson did was so damaging. He almost destroyed something I believe very deeply in.

I've tried for years to explain to my wife, who is not a sports fan, why sports are important. Why I am a fan. Why I care so much about Indiana basketball. Why I get upset when we lose. Why I yell and scream at the TV and call refs names they will never hear. Why I'm willing to drive from Chicago to Bloomington for every weekend home game on the schedule.

I've never been able to explain it to her, and maybe I never will, but this is as close as I've ever gotten.

Indiana basketball matters to me because it's something I share with people who matter to me, with people I grew up with, with my family (most of them, anyway). It matters to me because some of my best memories as a child are of watching IU basketball, and because I loved so much about my time as a student at IU. It matters because I feel a part of a community. It matters because I'm a part of something much bigger than myself.

I believe in Indiana basketball.

And because I do, I wanted to write this book, so that we don't forget how close we all came to having a program that we couldn't be proud of.

It's Indiana.

We're better than that.

www.ingramcontent.com/pod-product-compliance
Lightning Source LLC
Chambersburg PA
CBHW021049090426
42738CB00006B/257